THE
WEALTHY
Entrepreneur

The Formula for **MAKING MONEY** and
GAINING FINANCIAL CLARITY in Your Business

ROBERT GAUVREAU - FCPA

ISBN: 978-19-5-315335-7

Published by

If you are interested in publishing through Lifestyle Entrepreneurs Press, write to: *Publishing@LifestyleEntrepreneursPress.com*

Publications or foreign rights acquisition of our catalog books. Learn More: *www.LifestyleEntrepreneursPress.com*

Printed in the USA

Contents

CHAPTER 1

The Life of an Entrepreneur

*"Adversity causes some people to break;
others to break records."*
—William Ward

The term "entrepreneur" continues to gain attention as an exciting and financially rewarding career choice. However, there is significant risk associated with leaving a comfortable position with a guaranteed salary, benefits, and pension. What happens if it doesn't work out? Am I meant to be an entrepreneur? And is the risk of failing too much for me to handle?

Are you wondering if you have what it takes to be an entrepreneur? It really does take a special person to be able to put everything on the line for something they believe in. In order to understand whether you have what it takes, we need to first understand the characteristics of the entrepreneur.

1. **Growth-Oriented**

   The entrepreneur is not satisfied with staying in the status quo. They are constantly looking for new opportunities to improve their current situation, looking for opportunities to have increased impact in what they are doing. Entrepreneurs are looking for momentum in their lives, always wanting to push forward and not find themselves going backward.

2. Future-Focused

The entrepreneur is a visionary and is constantly looking into the future to see what is possible, how people are changing, and what can be offered to them to satisfy their needs. They are constantly dreaming of what is possible and have a real desire to create something that will have massive impact and will change the world.

3. Passionate

The entrepreneur gets excited about what it is that they deliver. Whether it is a new or innovative product or service, entrepreneurs are passionate about sharing with their customers what it is that they offer. The entrepreneur doesn't find what they are delivering to be work (although running some elements of their business may be a daunting concept).

4. Risk-Taker

The entrepreneur understands that there are risks associated with starting a business and creating a new product or service, some that require financial investment and some that require a tremendous time commitment. The entrepreneur understands that there are risks of failing, and they fully assume that responsibility, even though they want to find success in their business.

As you begin to understand the characteristics of being an entrepreneur, is this relatable to you? I am guessing that some, if not all, of the above characteristics are hitting home right now. In fact, you feel like I am describing you, and it all seems great. However, if you are already a fully invested entrepreneur, you are fully aware of the fact that is not all champagne and roses. In fact, being an entrepreneur is one of, if not the hardest positions you have ever held.

Here are some of the challenges associated with being an entrepreneur:

1. **No Cash**

   Many entrepreneurs find themselves puzzled when their accountants congratulate them for a great year. They owe tax money and it appears that they have made some great profits but have no money left. What happened? Something must be wrong.

2. **Lack of Savings**

   You have created a unique product or service, and it appears to be picking up. Demand is high, and you must continue to bring on additional team members and invest in new infrastructure, but you don't seem to be getting anything for yourself at the end of the day. There are no savings for your future, and you're not sure when you will be able to start building wealth. You are unsure of your financial future and how you will ever retire.

3. **Not Confident in your Financial Picture**

   You continue to operate your business on a day-to-day basis. Sometimes there is a good amount of cash in your bank account, but other times everything seems tight. Your sales continue to increase, but you're not sure how much money you're are making or how you improve this. You are unclear about how your business is financially performing.

The reality is, without a clear vision of where your business is heading, without understanding what the financial outcomes of that vision should look like, and without making sure you are on track to realize those financial outcomes, you are really heading into the future of your business with a significant financial unknown. Am I going to realize great financial results? Will I have enough savings to retire? Am I creating a business that is worth something? These are all questions that you need to have answered. In fact, without securing the financial position of your company, you lose focus on growing and creating a prosperous vision for your business. Financial stresses and uncertainties will prevent you from living your dream life and will prevent you from realizing financial freedom.

If you don't take control of your business now, clearly define your vision, understand your anticipated financial results, and stay accountable to those results, you could miss out on enjoying the rewards of time, impact in your business, and certainty of a financially rewarding future. With a 30% risk of failure within the first year and a 50% risk of failure within five years, the fear of failure and loss of time and investment continues to grow for entrepreneurs. Even if the business does survive, 83% of those businesses survive on a week-by-week basis, meaning that they are one week away from not making their rent or their payroll commitments.

Here is the good news: I have created an entrepreneurial framework that, when implemented in your business, will guarantee financial success, not only in your business, but in your life. It will provide you with confidence, direction, and a certain future of success. It will set you on the pathway to realizing the financial freedom you have wished for. Let's get started!

CHAPTER 2:

The Journey

"The way to get started is to quit talking and begin doing."
—Walt Disney

The greatest entrepreneurs of our time make business success look like a walk in the park. Here are three of my favourites:

Jeff Bezos, the founder and CEO of Amazon, has grown an e-commerce business to $233 billion dollars in annual revenue in 2018, which has caused massive disruption in the retail shopping industry and has soared Jeff into being the wealthiest man in the world, worth over $110 billion.

Elon Musk, the founder of SpaceX and the co-founder of Tesla (amongst other things), has grown Tesla motors to be one of the fastest growing automakers in the world with annual revenue of $21 billion dollars in 2018, while totally re-inventing the automobile industry by eliminating the longstanding dealership model and producing zero-emission battery vehicles that can drive long distances between charges. Not to mention that his company SpaceX is on a mission to revolutionize space technology and create recreational space travel.

Mark Zuckerberg, the co-founder of Facebook, has created a social media and social networking service that has connected billions of people across the world. Facebook has grown to $62 billion in annual revenue in 2018, and has completely changed the way in which people communicate and stay connected with each other.

Here's the problem: we only see on the surface what they have accomplished rather than the struggles, financial hardships, failures, and stresses that they needed to overcome along the way ... and believe me, there have been many! For example, in 2014, Jeff Bezos invested $170 million dollars into creating the Amazon Fire smartphone. Within months, the price of the phone dropped from $199 to being sold for under a dollar (with a two-year AT&T contract). The phone was quickly discontinued, and Amazon lost their $170 million investment. In 2008, Elon Musk and his two companies, SpaceX and Tesla, were both on the verge of bankruptcy. In the same year, Musk declared personal bankruptcy to prevent the companies from imploding. Musk cites this as the worst year of his life, when everything he touched (including his personal finances) were failing or were on the verge of failure. And in 2018, Facebook was infiltrated by Russian operatives, and the Cambridge Analytica scandal began with concerns about users' psychological well-being. Not to mention that Facebook lost $123 billion in value in one week alone. The reality is that so many entrepreneurs experience struggles, financial hardships, failures, and stress, and although there may be moments of glory, there are also many moments where times get tough.

I remember the day I decided I was going to start my own business. I was in my mid-twenties, I had just recently received my Chartered Professional Accountant (CPA) designation, I was working at a well-respected national accounting firm, and I had a massive void in my life. I wasn't doing what I was meant to do, and I was on a mission to find it.

In my senior accountant role, I was pushed into the audit world. Not the ugly auditor who comes in from the government to tell you that they are going through your life's financial affairs and to collect your tax money, but rather an independent auditor who would go into non-profit organizations such as hospitals, municipalities, school boards, and charitable organizations to make sure that their financial reporting was accurate and complete. This auditing is a requirement for many of these organizations so that they can continue to receive government funding and stay in business to provide the essential services our communities need.

The problem was, these organizations had accountants who were doing a great job, and I was essentially there to provide my seal of approval. I wasn't adding any perceived value for the organizations to become better at what they do, or to help them add more value to our community ... and then it hit me. I had an extensive financial knowledge of how businesses operate, and I needed to find how I could offer this knowledge to help those who could benefit from this. In the early part of my financial career, I spent my time working with entrepreneurs and helping them with tax planning and understanding the cash flow of their businesses. I loved this work, and I was contributing to the financial success of their businesses, but I had no idea how to run a business ... and that was going to change. At the end of 2007 I quit my job and headed out on my own, into the scary and lonely world of entrepreneurship!

As I was starting to plan out the future of my business, I went in to see a local business account manager at the bank, with my business plan prepared, a professional designation behind me, and a mission to change the world for entrepreneurs. I will never forget this experience. I was greeted by an older gentleman who asked me to have a seat. It was hard to see his face, because he had a newspaper up to the top of his eyes, but I could certainly see his shiny black dress shoes since they were nicely crossed on the desk in front of him. Behind the paper I heard the question, "How do you think I am going to be able to loan you money?" This seemed strange ... I had projected financial statements showing profits, a professional designation that was highly demanded, and a full business plan, not to mention a serious amount of passion for working with my chosen clients. I was ready! What I was not ready for was for rejection to occur so quickly. I had failed. I was laughed out of the bank manager's office and told "good luck" in a very sarcastic tone! I felt defeated. I had failed. I was trying to ask for help from the wrong people. But the truth was, I didn't know who the right people were. However, I was persistent. I did find another bank that believed in what I was doing, and it fully funded me to get started ... and so the journey began.

I remember the first few years – there were so many challenges:

- Cash flow was tight
- I was working 100+ hours a week
- I was struggling to build a team as fast as I was growing
- I was continuously reinvesting with nothing left for myself

Although there were many struggles, I knew I had a passion to help entrepreneurs create financial success in their lives. And as I continued down the entrepreneurial journey of starting my own business, I was learning all the tough lessons that came along with running a business. Although it was costly, I was learning what worked and what didn't firsthand. I was learning how to better guide an entrepreneur toward realizing success in their business.

Over the years, my work with entrepreneurs was gaining attention. I was admitted into fellowship of the CPA program (that is a lifetime achievement award for advancing the profession), and I was recognized with entrepreneurship awards, professional services awards, and leadership awards. I was being recognized for what I created in the business community and amongst my peers.

In 2015, one of the most interesting things happened. I received a call from a representative of Tony Robbins. Tony was looking to recruit me and my team to work with him and his entrepreneur clients who attend his popular business mastery event. *What?!* One of the greatest global entrepreneurial minds wanted my team's expertise to add value to his clients? Let's just say I couldn't say no. For three years I joined Tony at his business mastery events as a partner in his Global Accounting Advisors program. I had the pleasure to study his teachings and work with him and his clients to create a world class advisory program for his attendees.

I have created a multimillion-dollar accounting firm that specialized in working with entrepreneurs to create extraordinary financial results in their businesses. I have built an incredible team of professionals and I have built tools and tips to help entrepreneurs with all aspects of their businesses. I have lived the ups and downs of being an entrepreneur and have had the pleasure to work with some of the world's greatest entrepreneurs to deeply understand the inner workings of how to create a financially successful business.

As an entrepreneur, business strategist, and financial expert who works with over 500 entrepreneurs across North America, I have helped business owners create their vision, execute their goals, and create extraordinary financial results in their own lives. My goal is to help as many entrepreneurs realize financial freedom as I can. This is why I have created the Vision to Results financial framework, and this is why I want to share it with you in this book, so that you have all of the tools you require to create financial freedom in your own life.

When we think of financial freedom, we think of doing what we want, when we want, with who we want, but it goes far beyond this. By achieving financial freedom in your life, you will have clarity around your business and personal finances, you will have accumulated enough wealth to never have to worry about money again, and you will be able to focus on the true joy that life can bring, whatever that looks like for you. This is my wish for you.

CHAPTER 3:

Vision to Results

"Be the change you wish to see in the world."
—Mahatma Gandhi

As you may have picked up on in the previous chapter, I am very passionate about helping entrepreneurs realize financial freedom in their lives. I love working with entrepreneurs for a multitude of reasons. Why? You are passionate, you take risks, you invest in yourself and your business, you are willing to try new things, you are growth-oriented, and your ideas and solutions are truly changing the world one day at a time. I love working with entrepreneurs because I know my financial frameworks and expertise can allow for their businesses to create extraordinary financial results, which in turn will allow them to have a greater impact in their business and have a bigger part in changing the world. This is what gets me excited every single day: knowing that I am doing my part to help people like you change the world.

Here's the good news: the risk of failure as an entrepreneur can be all but eliminated if you ensure that the financial foundation of your business is planned for, expectations are outlined, and the financial results are consistently monitored. This is the Vision to Results framework that I have called the entrepreneur's formula for making money and gaining financial clarity, and I am ready to share it with you now.

Before we get started, you need to understand that this framework needs to be followed in sequence. Although each of the steps in the framework could be individually implemented, the key to maximizing the results of the implementation would be to start at the beginning and complete each step along the way in the order they are presented. Now let's start by looking at each of the individual steps involved within the framework.

Step 1: Start with the End in Mind

Successful entrepreneurs have a clearly defined vision as to where they want to go with their business. They understand how much money they want to make, they understand what they want to accomplish, they understand the impact that they want to have with their business, and they understand the resources that are necessary in order to accomplish this vision.

Not only does the successful entrepreneur clearly define this vision, but the entire team, who are contributors of the success of the business, is fully aware of the direction they are heading and what their roles are in achieving these goals. The more clearly each team member understands their role, the more likely it is that the team will accomplish their goals together.

In the Start with the End in Mind chapter (Chapter 4), we will focus on the necessary components of outlining a vision and understanding the goals of your organization. We will then walk through the process of documenting these goals so that they will establish a basis for how we create the projects necessary to accomplish the goals of your organization. We will also establish financial goals for the next twelve months, the next three years, and the next ten years.

Step 2: Understanding Your Business Financial Model

In order for a business to be successful, it is imperative that the entrepreneur understand what the desired profit is, what the costs associated with generating these profits are, and what revenue needs to be delivered in order for the overall profits to be realized.

Successful entrepreneurs need to understand the profitability related to the product or service they are delivering to their clients, what the impacts to that profitability are should the volume of revenue increase or decrease, what the fixed costs associated with delivering this revenue look like, and what types of resources need to be brought in to ensure the quality is delivered to the customer.

In the Understanding Your Financial Model chapter (Chapter 5), we will focus on understanding how the financial model of your business is structured, how any changes to the volume of revenue will impact the profitability of your business, and what the break-even of your business is to know the minimum requirements in order to start profiting in your business.

Step 3: Predicting Financial Results

You may be aware of different terminology related to predicting financial results, such as forecasted financial statements, budgeting process, etc. This is where we take the vision/goals of your business, with the understanding of the businesses financial model, and create the required financial outcomes of your business in order to generate these goals.

In order to operate a successful business, the entrepreneur needs to understand and visually see the end result. In fact, how can a business owner know if they are on track to reaching their goals if their goals aren't outlined ahead of time? This is one of the key elements to achieving extraordinary results in your business.

In the Predicting Financial Results chapter (Chapter 6), we will walk through the process of how to determine what the key numbers are within your business, including (but not limited to) the operational income and revenue, and everything in between. This outline will end up being the desired financial results of your business and will outline the level of growth necessary to achieve these results.

Step 4: Outline the Key Outcomes – One at a Time

Once you have outlined the high-level financial objectives for your organization through the budgeting process, you need to outline the individual metrics that need to be achieved for the budgeted financial results to be realized.

Successful entrepreneurs break down these key metrics and have individuals on their teams accountable for achieving these benchmarks. If you really want to drive a culture of growth and success, you need to ensure that everyone on your team has a number that they are responsible for. This number may be shared amongst a team, but everyone should be responsible for driving a key metric. If all of the individuals on your team are working toward achieving these metrics, and if they are all met, then the business will meet its predicted financial results.

In the Outlining Key Outcomes chapter (Chapter 7), we will review what these key metrics look like, and discuss them in detail so that you will be able to fully understand what goes into creating these individual goals for the team.

Step 5: Create a Scoreboard

One of the greatest mistakes entrepreneurs make is not implementing a system to track their financial progress and results. Far too often, business owners do not put a focus on having an up-to-date understanding of how their business is performing financially. If you don't know how the business is performing, how will you know if you are on track to realizing the financial results you are hoping for?

I often hear from entrepreneurs new to working with our team that the last time they reviewed the financial performance of their company was when they met with their accountant, and at that time they were reviewing information that was out of date by over six months. Traditionally, accountants have focused on historical information, which does provide a good base of what to expect in the future; however, it does not tell you where you are at right now, and what needs to be adjusted to ensure you are financially successful.

In the Creating a Scoreboard chapter (Chapter 8), we will identify the benefits related to having up-to-date financial information, how to implement a system that will provide you with this information, and how to track your key metrics that drive the performance of your business.

Step 6: Stay Accountable

Have you ever heard that if you put an idea out into the universe and shout it from the rooftops for everyone to hear, it seems to suddenly happen? There are many psychological studies that show that when you share your goals with others, especially if you say you are going to do something, that you have greater internal motivation and accountability to yourself to achieve these results.

Great entrepreneurs set out their vision, they share it with their team, they have their team understand what they need to do to contribute to this vision, they track the progress, and they hold each other accountable to these goals. As a business owner, you can have internal and/or external accountability partners to ensure you, as the visionary, are kept accountable to your goals.

In the Staying Accountable chapter (Chapter 9), we will discuss the accountability process inside your business and how to ensure your team will stay accountable to achieving their metrics. We will discuss how to implement a regular meeting schedule, the topics and agenda that need to be included in these meetings, and how to make the most of your time. No entrepreneur wants to fill up their schedule with unnecessary meetings; however, we will introduce a system and how to make these accountability sessions as efficient as possible to drive real results.

Step 7: Grow Your Business

To some entrepreneurs, growing a business seems like a daunting task. In fact, many entrepreneurs just want to be the expert who is creating the product or service and are unsure how to effectively turn that product or service into a growing business. The good news here is that growing the business, specifically growing the revenue related to a business, is quite simple – at least in theory.

Great businesses understand strategic opportunities, the demand of the market, and how to take advantage of these opportunities when they arise.

In the Growing Your Business chapter (Chapter 10), we will focus on the three ways a business can grow its revenue, will drill down in those three areas to really understand what they mean, and will provide you with specific actionable items you can implement to grow your business today.

Step 8: Maximize Your Profits

The ultimate goal of starting on the entrepreneurial journey is to have a massive impact and to make money doing something that you love. And let me tell you right up front, the more money you make, the more impact you can have, and the less stress and anxiousness you will have along your journey. In other words, creating a business that generates serious profits will maximize your entrepreneurial experience!

A very important component of profit maximization that needs to be understood is that you don't necessarily need to increase your revenue to increase your profits. Too many entrepreneurs focus on revenue generation as the only means to increase profits. In fact, many entrepreneurs spin their wheels in the mud by investing all their time in growing revenue, when a focus on cost management and structure optimization may be a more effective way to increase the profitability of the business. The ideal scenario is to ensure that your financial house is in order, that the business is running as efficiently as possible and is ready to scale, and then you can go all in on revenue generation and growing the top line of the business. Then, and only then, will you be building a business machine that will maximize profits.

In the Profit Maximization chapter (Chapter 11), we will focus on how we eliminate excessive costs, complete a review of the financial model, review expenditure categories that are prone to inefficiency, and learn how to analyze the profits of a business to determine if the results are good or exceptional. In essence, we will look at the business and come up with a plan to implement extraordinary financial results.

Step 9: Optimize Your Cash Flow

One of the biggest barriers to a successful business is focusing all your attention on profits and not paying attention to the cash flow of the business. Although profit is essential in a business, if you have no cash to reinvest in future growth or if you can't afford to continue to deliver your product or service, then profits are useless.

Successful entrepreneurs have a great handle on the cash requirements and cash resources available within their business. It is essential, if you want to grow your business and create extraordinary financial results, that you understand the tools and techniques available to maximize your cash flow. As the old saying goes, cash is king ... and it is very true in your business.

In the Understanding Cash Flow chapter (Chapter 12), we will discuss different ways that profit is different from cash and how to structure your business to best maximize your cash resources, and I will provide tools and tricks that can be implemented to take your business cash flow to an all new positive level.

Step 10: Minimize Your Taxes

As the founding partner of a CPA firm, I can assure you that the tax pain for entrepreneurs is very real. Wouldn't it be amazing if we didn't have to worry about taxes? In fact, it seems like the government always has their hands in our pockets, and it always seems like what we owe is more than it should be.

There are many elements that go into ensuring that you are minimizing your tax burden. What I will say is that successful entrepreneurs invest in proactive methods to mitigate future taxes so that they can reduce the tax burden and balances owed to the government and actively reinvest their proceeds into growing their businesses and/or generating massive wealth. What I can tell you is that a significant number of entrepreneurs are paying excessive amounts of tax, and if this is not optimized, are giving money away that they could use in a more meaningful way.

In the Minimize Your Taxes chapter (Chapter 13), we will be discussing the optimal business structures available to you and how different compensation strategies can impact how much tax you pay, and will dive deep into the cost of paying too much tax. Let's just say after this chapter, you should have a really good grasp on whether you are utilizing all opportunities available to minimize your tax burden.

Step 11: Build Your Wealth

Once you create a business that is generating extraordinary results, it is time to build wealth. This may involve reinvesting in business assets, revenue generation strategies so as to increase the enterprise value of the business, having cash or related investments inside the company should the operations need a boost in the future, or deter-mining how we utilize the performance of the business to maximize the wealth of the entrepreneur personally. An optimal strategy may involve all four, but however you decide you want to optimize your wealth generation, we need to have a plan in place.

Successful entrepreneurs have a clearly defined vision for their personal wealth, including how much money they will need should they decide to focus on moving away from the daily operations of the business. The reality is, no investment will generate the return or income that a successful business will provide; however, the goal would be to start building multiple income streams that will gener-ate enough income so that should you decide to exit the business, all of your finances are in place to live life without having to worry about affording it.

In the Building Wealth chapter (Chapter 14), we will discuss the power of forced savings, investment opportunities, personal budgeting, designing the future of your dreams, and building true financial freedom.

This is the vision to success – the entrepreneur's formula for making money and gaining financial clarity. If you implement these steps in your business, you will guarantee yourself extraordinary financial results, and will be well on your way to delivering a greater impact and building a life of financial freedom. Are you ready to roll up your sleeves and get started? I can't wait to share this with you!

CHAPTER 4:

Start with the End in Mind

"If you can dream it, you can do it."
—Walt Disney

When you think of the greatest companies in history, you think of organizations like Walt Disney Company, Apple, Microsoft, Tesla, Facebook, Amazon, and many more. The one thing that all these extraordinarily successful companies have in common is that they are very clear on who they are and what they want to deliver.

Let's take the Walt Disney Company for example. The mission of the Walt Disney Company is to "entertain, inform and inspire people around the globe through the power of unparalleled story-telling, reflecting the iconic brands, creative minds and innovative technologies that make ours the world's premier entertainment company." As is evident, the Walt Disney Company is very clear on who they are and what they want to deliver to their target market. This has been the foundation to the company's long-term success as a global leader in the entertainment business.

Unless you are very clear on where you want to go, how do you know how to get there?

The first step in generating extraordinary results is being very clear on the outcomes that you desire as an entrepreneur. What do you desire for your business? What do you desire for yourself personally? These goals can be both qualitative and quantitative in nature. I like to refer to this step as the goal-setting session.

Goal-Setting Session

To begin the goal-setting session, you need to be in an uninterrupted space, preferably one that is away from your phone and has you inaccessible from other obligations and unscheduled interruptions. This is dedicated time you must spend working on your business. It is imperative that you can focus this time on really understanding who you are, what you want to accomplish, and how you intend to accomplish this. Depending on how your business is currently structured, this can be an exercise with your key management team, or it can be an exercise that you complete by yourself, as the entrepreneurial visionary defining the vision for the business. In the past, I have completed this exercise alone and then brought in my management team to see if we were all on the same page as to what we wanted to accomplish. It was incredibly valuable to complete this with my management team as I could see how well I had previously relayed my vision for the company. In most cases when the process is completed individually first, and then with the management team, there is misalignment in vision, and the process of working through this as a team instead creates massive buy-in from those responsible for executing the vision of the organization.

To begin, we need to introduce the 3 P's of goal setting: *Purpose, People, and Positioning*

Purpose

The very first step of the goal-setting session is to get very clear on your reason for being in business and to specifically identify why you do what you do. People have often referred to this as a mission statement or a vision statement; however, I like to think of this as your purpose. In Simon Sinek's book *Start with Why*, he discusses how, "People don't buy what you do. They buy why you do it." This suggests that understanding your why, or knowing your organization's purpose, is integral to outlining where you see your business going. If you don't know what your clear purpose as an organization is, how can you expect others to figure it out?

Here are some questions to think of as you get very specific and clear on your purpose:

- Why was your company started?
- Why does the company exist now?
- What does your company deliver (product or service)?
- What does the customer want from the company?
- Why do people care about your company?
- What problems are you solving?

As an example of getting very clear on purpose, my company, Gauvreau & Associates CPA, was created to help entrepreneurs realize extraordinary financial results. We do this because we have a specialized financial expertise that entrepreneurs need to deliver their mission with greater impact through improved financial results.

Once you become clear on why you do what you do, you can move toward getting clear on who you are as a business.

People

I like to think of this as "the way we do things around here," or the culture of the business. These are the values of the individuals who make up your team, which attract like-minded individuals and push away those who don't have a good fit. By understanding the culture of the business and ensuring that you have members on your team who have aligned values, you create a sense of identity and a passion for delivering that value to your customers. The best part of having a clearly defined culture is that once a team member understands it, they can't wait to come to work every day.

- What are the unwritten rules embraced by those who are on your team?
- Who are you as a group?
- What values are most important to your team?
- What characteristics do you look for in a new team member?
- How would you want external people to perceive you?

Having a clearly defined culture or "way we do things around here" is imperative to the future success of your business. As the visionary and leader of the organization, it is your responsibility to ensure that everyone is on the same page, both from a purpose perspective and from a values perspective. The more aligned your team, the more effectively they will execute the vision of the organization. The goal of this process is to come up with three or four key words that describe you as an organization.

This is an incredible exercise to perform with your team. I will never forget when I brought my management team in to complete this process. The energy level was extremely high, and it took a while to narrow the "who we are" down to three words. However, when we completed the exercise, we were extremely united, and the excitement to portray these three words to the rest of our team and to our customers was incredible. We were aligned like we never had been in the past. We were proud to be known for "People, passion, integrity."

Positioning

The positioning of the organization is really the understanding of what the business's competitive advantage is. According to Harvard Business School professor Michael Porter's book *Competitive Advantage*, there are really four ways to achieve competitive advantage.

1. **Cost Leadership**

   Cost leadership refers to a company who provides reasonable value at a low price. These tend to be companies who enter into an established industry but are trying to beat their competition by charging less for what they deliver. This tends to be a business that has a focus on maximizing volume with an emphasis on efficiency in operations.

2. **Cost Focus**

   A focus or niche down strategy refers to a company who provides services to a very specific industry and has unique knowledge of this industry. In a cost focus, because of the organization's knowledge and expertise in a specified market, they can deliver the product or service in a more efficient manner. In this case, they can utilize a lower price and still make profit due to the efficiency of their delivery.

3. **Differentiation**

   Differentiation refers to a company who can deliver better or more unique results for its customers. It is typically referred to as an "innovator" and tends to be the first to the market in its specialized field. A business can achieve differentiation by providing a unique or high-quality service or product. A company who creates competitive advantage by differentiation does things differently than their competition, focuses on exceptional quality and/or service, typically charges higher prices, and generates more profit on what it delivers.

4. Differentiation Focus

As mentioned above, a focus or niche down strategy refers to a company who provides services to a very specific industry and has knowledge unique to this industry. In a differentiation focus, a company can deliver their expert, specialized product or service to their niche market, but also do it by focusing on delivering exceptional quality and/or services and can typically charge the highest prices due to the experience they deliver with their specialized knowledge.

What is your current competitive advantage? Are you differentiated from everyone else (are you unique)? Are you a low-price alternative? Are you a niche provider? These are all questions you need to answer to understand your strategic advantage over your competition.

To continue with the example of my firm, we have positioned ourselves as a differentiation focus provider. We work with a specific group, entrepreneurs, and we focus on delivering a unique quality experience compared to the traditional accounting firm. For example, most accounting firms provide audits to non-profits, municipalities, etc., and prepare financial statements and tax returns for small business. We have focused specifically on providing services to the entrepreneur. We provide financial statements and tax returns, but all our time and attention are focused around the entrepreneur. With that said, due to that specialized expertise, we are able to provide a very unique service offering, working closely with entrepreneurs not only to assist them with taxes and accounting, but assisting them with understanding their internal goals, how to execute those goals, and how to generate extraordinary financial results.

Ten-Year Vision

> *"Start small, think big. Don't worry about too many things at once. Take a handful of simple things to begin with, and then progress to more complex ones. Think about not just tomorrow, but the future. Put a ding in the universe."*
>
> —Steve Jobs

As the first part of the goal session is complete, which is understanding your purpose, people, and positioning, you should now have a united vision of who you are, the values you live by, and the way you have defined the strategic advantage of your business. Now we go big! Let's start with defining what the ten-year vision is for your business. This is considered a brainstorming session, so the best way to get started would be to start writing down answers to the following questions (and anything else you would consider relevant for where you see your company in ten years):

- What will the name of your business be (same)?
- Where will your business be located?
- What will your business sell and/or what services will it deliver?
- Will you have multiple locations?

- What demographic are you serving?
- Will you be delivering across the globe? Nationally?
- What does your revenue look like?
- What do your profits look like?
- What is your role in the business? Are you still an active leader? Or have you moved into an investor role?
- How many employees do you have?
- Do you have an element of your business that is online?
- What does your client communication look like? Are you using a CRM? Are you maximizing your communication on social media channels?
- How are you marketing your business?
- What type of professional development are you invested in?
- How quickly can you obtain relevant financial information to make strategic decisions?
- How much are you reinvesting in growing your business?
- How many clients do you have?
- How are you positioned in relation to your competition?
- What are your three to five words that will define the culture of your business?
- How big will your management team be?
- Are you bringing in specialist knowledge such as human resources, finance, and legal?
- How much money do you have in investments?
- How much are you taking out of the business on a regular basis?
- Where will you be living?
- What kind of car will you be driving?
- How often will you take vacations?
- Will you have any family working in your business?

- Will you have a succession plan outlined?
- Will your children be in post-secondary education? Private school? Getting married and having children?
- Any other relevant questions you feel you should ask yourself

Once you answer the above questions, you should be feeling excited about the possibilities of the future. In one of my favourite books of all time, *Good to Great* by Jim Collins and Jerry Porras, they refer to the ten-year goals as a BHAG, or "big, hairy, audacious goals." Not only did the most successful companies identify that they were doing ten-year planning, but the book also noted that the majority of the greatest companies were completing up to twenty-five-year planning, demonstrating where they saw the vision of the company heading over the next twenty-five-year period. In my personal experience though, entrepreneurs are already chasing butterflies and thinking of the next new idea, so I don't feel that we need to predict what your company looks like in twenty-five years, mostly because we can't really predict the political and environmental climates that our businesses will be living in. The reality is, predicting the next ten years of your business will be far enough into the future to identify your ultimate hopes and dreams for the business. Now, let's start making this more of a reality.

Three-Year Vision

"If you don't know where you are going, you'll end up someplace else."

—Yogi Berra

Now that you have looked out at your ten-year vision, it should be very clear what your ultimate goals look like. What your dreams look like. What the perfect business looks like. So why don't you create a plan to start realizing that business? Why wouldn't you, really? At the end of the day, you are in charge of creating your own destiny.

The next step is looking at the three-year vision. Although many people have difficulty envisioning exactly where their business will be in ten years, where the business will be in three years is right around the corner. In fact, we are only a few good years away from realizing these results. Contrary to the many big picture questions of the ten-year vision, we are going to get a little more specific with the three-year vision. With this exercise, we want to get more specific, more measurable, and more realistic with our expectations of where your business will be. By keeping our ten-year vision in mind, we should identify what we need to do within the next three-year period in order to realize our goals. Let's start by answering the following questions:

- What will your annual revenue be?
- How many employees will you need to add in order to deliver that revenue? What will their salary costs look like?
- Will you need to add any salespeople? Admin people?
- Will your market be expanding or contracting?
- What will your competition look like? Will this impact the need for your marketing efforts to be adjusted in order to hit your revenue targets?
- Will you need to invest in any infrastructure to deliver this revenue?
- How much money will the company make?
- How much money will be going toward investments?

- How much money will you be taking out as owner compensation?
- Any other relevant questions you feel need to be answered

Now that you have gone through this exercise, you should feel a little clearer as to where your business is heading. In fact, you can see that these results are achievable, especially if you have a specific list of objectives that need to be accomplished. Your team is aligned, energized, and excited about the possibilities of hitting these targets. This just got real!

One-Year Vision

"By failing to prepare, you are preparing to fail."
—Benjamin Franklin

Now that you have outlined what your three-year vision looks like, and you have a clear vision of where you want to get to over the next three-year period, you can back that up into what needs to get accomplished in the next twelve months and what benchmarks you need to hit to get from where you are now to where you want to be in three years. Even think of the ten-year vision and what you want to accomplish in that period. What needs to happen now in order for you to reach your future vision for the company? As was the case in the previous exercises, we want to outline what objectives need to be met over the next twelve months to realize your one-year vision. In this exercise, you need to be realistic in your expectations for yourself, and you need to outline objectives that are attainable. However, if you think you can do it, push the limits! Let's start by answering the following questions:

- What will your annual revenue be for this period?

- Will you need to hire anyone in the next twelve months?

- What additional costs will you incur in order to achieve the next twelve months' revenue targets?

- What marketing investment will you need to incur to realize your revenue targets?

- Do you need to adjust the delivery of your product or services?

- Do you need to improve your customer service?

- Should you be introducing a CRM platform? Adjusting your client communication?

- How many new clients will you need?

- Are there any new products or services you need to deliver?

- Do you need to implement a new financial reporting process so that you can measure your progress?

- What will your tax obligations look like during this period?

- What obstacles are in the way of you achieving your goals for the next twelve months?

- Are there any other specific objectives you need to meet during the next twelve months?

- Any other relevant questions you feel need to be answered

Congratulations. You have now just outlined the major targets that your organization needs to hit during the next twelve months. This has outlined your one-year vision. At this point, you may be excited, but you may also be skeptical of what you are setting yourself up for. No need to worry about any second thoughts at this point. When we get to the next chapter, we will resolve any concerns you have for the one-year vision.

CHAPTER 5:

Understanding Your Financial Model

*"An entrepreneur tends to bite off
a little more than he can chew hoping
he'll quickly learn how to chew it."*
—Roy Ash

The exciting part of being an entrepreneur is being able to create something new, come up with a new idea, and dream about how this new concept will potentially change the world. Entrepreneurs have an incredible ability to see things others don't, to see the future being changed, and to see how they can have a greater impact on what they deliver. However, one of the limitations to being so big picture focused is that you lose sight of where you are now, and what you need to do to realize those big vision ideas in a way that provides positive financial results. In order to move your new concept forward, you must have an idea of what your current and future financial model looks like.

In a simplified approach to understanding your financial model, there are three elements: revenue, variable costs, and fixed costs. In addition to these three elements, there are three other financial concepts that you need to understand: gross profit, operational income, and the break-even point. Let's discuss each of these concepts here.

Revenue

Understanding the income sources of your business is the simplest of the three components of an organization's earnings. Revenue represents the income your business receives from business-related activities. Sources of revenue could include (but are not limited to) the following:

- Sale of goods
- Delivering services
- Investment income (rental, dividends, interest, capital gains, etc.)

Each type of revenue involves different financial elements and can either be a one-time sale of a product or service or a reoccurring transaction. As an aside, if you are able to build a company that is based on a reoccurring revenue model (such as membership fees/ subscriptions), the value of your business will increase due to the reliability of the future earnings and outcomes of the business. The more reliable your future revenue is, the higher the value you would be able to command for a potential sale of your business.

Variable Costs (or Direct Costs)

Variable costs are expenses that are incurred by the business that change in direct proportion to the revenue that is being delivered. In simpler terms, variable costs are the direct costs related to delivering a product or service to the end user. It is important to note that the variable costs associated with selling a good will be completely different than the costs associated with delivering a service. Understanding your variable costs is essential to predicting the financial future of your business. By understanding the direct costs associated with delivering your revenue, you will have clarity around how many items the business will need to sell to become profitable. We will look at three unique business models that will have different variable costs to gain a better understanding of how this works:

1. Service Provider

In a service-based industry, there are no direct product costs that are tied to the delivery of a service. There may be supplies costs that a service provider needs, but there is no good that is being sold during this process. Here are some examples of what variable costs may be involved for a service provider business:

- Wages and benefits (directly related to those delivering the service – does not include fixed salaries of the executives, administration, IT, HR, finance, etc.)
- Supplies required to deliver the service
- Other direct sales costs (such as commissions, lead acquisition costs, etc.)
- Vehicle costs (travel to deliver the service)

2. Sale of Goods (reseller model – retail or wholesale)

In a business where you are buying product and reselling it for a profit, and when you are a distributor of the product, you will have some different variable costs associated with the derivation of your revenue. Here are some examples of what variable costs may be involved for a reseller model business:

- Product purchases
- Packaging
- Wages and benefits (directly related to the product sale/ delivery)
- Supplies directly related to the delivery of the product
- Shipping
- Other direct sales costs (such as commissions, lead acquisition costs, etc.)
- Vehicle costs (travel to deliver or sell the product)

3. Sale of Goods (manufacturing)

When a business is creating a product or material that it will sell to either an end user or a wholesale distributor, the variable costs associated with generating these revenues can be a little bit more complicated. Here are some examples of what variable costs may be included for a manufacturing model business:

- Purchase of raw materials
- Direct labour for assembly
- Packaging
- Wages and benefits (directly related to the product sale/ delivery)
- Supplies directly related to the delivery of the product
- Shipping
- Other direct sales costs (such as commissions, lead acquisition costs, etc.)
- Vehicle costs (travel to deliver or sell the product)

- Variable overhead costs (this includes the cost of heat, hydro, water, etc., that can be directly attributed to the cost of manufacturing a unit being produced)

It is imperative that you consider all the specific costs that will increase or decrease with the manufacturing, sale, and delivery of a product or service. The better you understand the variable costs associated to delivering your revenue, the better you will be able to predict how many units you need to sell in order to generate the profitability necessary to realize your vision.

Fixed Costs (or Indirect Costs)

Fixed costs are relatively straight forward. A fixed cost is a cost that does not change over the short-term, even if a business experiences changes in its sales volume or other activity levels. If your revenue increases, your fixed costs will remain fixed. Understanding what your fixed costs are is essential to understanding how much net revenue you need to generate to cover the costs to operate your business. Here are some examples of what fixed costs may be required to operate your business:

- Rent
- Indirect wages and benefits (management, administration, IT, HR, finance, and any compensation that is required to be paid irrespective of the sales volume)
- Advertising (generic – more brand related and not determined to be a cost of acquisition)
- Bank charges
- Insurance
- Interest

- Professional development
- Professional fees
- Property taxes
- Telephone
- Travel expenses
- Utilities
- Vehicle (if not directly tied to delivering product or services)

When trying to understand what future profitability will look like in your business, you will need to have a complete understanding of the costs that will be involved in order to open the doors. This does not say that the fixed costs of your business will not increase over time. In fact, as your business continues to grow, the chances are it will need a larger facility, which will require more rent. When your business grows, it may have to expand its management and administrative team. It may have an increase in its equipment, which may have increased insurance costs associated with it. All of these expenses may change as your business evolves; however, they will not increase based on delivering one additional product or service to your customers. They may change if you continue to grow over the longer term.

Gross Profit/Gross Profit Margin (or Gross Margin)

Gross profit is one of the most important elements of understanding your financial model. The gross profit is the profit a company makes after deducting the costs associated with making and selling its products, or the costs associated with providing its services. In other words, it is calculated as revenue minus variable costs. This is why you need to be very clear on your revenue and the costs directly related with delivering that revenue, so that you can calculate your gross profit. Even more important than understanding the gross profit is understanding the gross profit margin (or gross margin). The gross profit margin is calculated as the percentage of profit as a percentage of the revenue target. An example of this is as follows:

A business sells computers that it purchases from a wholesale provider. The company sells the computers for $1,000 and purchases them from their provider for $600. Note: this is the total cost required to deliver the computer to the end user. The gross profit on selling an individual computer is $400, resulting in the gross profit margin on this transaction being 40% ($400/$1,000). As a business continues to grow, the gross profit will increase; however, the gross profit percentage will stay the same (unless you are reducing your per unit sale price, or your costs increase). Continuing with the same example above, imagine that the company now sells two computers.

Computer sale	$2,000
Cost of computer	$1,200
Gross profit	$800
Gross profit percentage	40%

As you can see from the above example, the more the company sells, the more the gross profit increases; however, the gross profit percentage remains stable.

Operating Income

Operating income is income earned within a business after all expenses are considered (except income tax and extraordinary items that are atypical to the operations of the business). In other words, operating income is calculated as revenue, less variable costs, less fixed costs. This is also referred to as the business profit, or the bottom-line profit of the business. To provide clarity, let's continue with the example above. In our example, the company sells two computers for $2,000 in total. Let's assume that the business pays $500 in rent and pays $200 for business insurance. The example is as follows:

Revenue - Sale of computers	$ 2,000.00
Variable costs	
- cost of computers	$ 1,200.00
Gross profit	$ 800.00
Fixed costs	
- insurance	$ 200.00
- rent	$ 500.00
Operating income	$ 100.00

In this example, the operating income is calculated as $100, which demonstrates a positive bottom-line profitability of the business. However, what if we go back to the first example, when the company only sells one computer? The result of only one sale is as follows:

Revenue - Sale of computers	$ 1,000.00
Variable costs	
- cost of computers	$ 600.00
Gross profit	$ 400.00
Fixed costs	
- insurance	$ 200.00
- rent	$ 500.00
Operating income	$ 100.00

In our secondary example, the business is losing money and is in financial trouble. However, in both examples, the fixed costs did not change. The use of this example shows how fixed costs, the costs required to have the doors open in the business, need to be covered by the profits in a business for the operating income of the business to be positive.

Break-Even Point

The break-even point of a business is where total revenue equals total costs. This means that the revenue less variable costs (which is the gross profit) is equal to the fixed costs. The operational income at the break-even point is zero. See the break-even analysis diagram below:

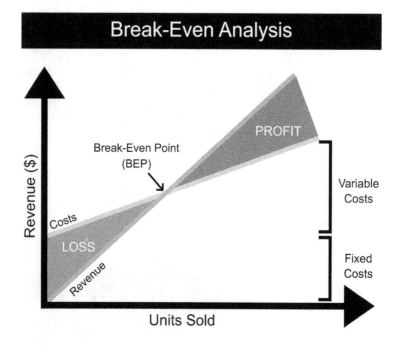

Understanding the break-even point of the operations is essential to the foundation of creating financial success in your business. The break-even point provides you with the following information:

- The number of units that you need to sell to cover all costs
- The revenue total that you need to surpass to create a financially sustainable business
- A bottom-line benchmark for revenue targets
- The ability to predict the effect of changes in revenue
- The ability to analyze the relationship between fixed and variable costs

So many entrepreneurs go into their businesses without knowing their break-even target. Without knowing what your break-even point is, you don't know what your minimum required revenue or unit sales needs to be to succeed with your venture. If you outline this up front, you can ensure that it appears reasonable and that you can at a minimum accomplish this target; otherwise you need to adjust your financial model, whether it be eliminating some of the fixed costs of the business or determining how to increase the gross profit percentage on your individual sales.

Once you have gone through the exercise of outlining your revenue streams and the specific costs related to delivering that revenue, and understanding what the fixed costs will be for your business to open the doors, you will have a clear understanding of the financial model of your business. You will understand the minimum performance for your business to successfully operate, and you will understand how the profitability of the business can be impacted by adjusting the revenue targets. At this point, you are set to outline what your financial targets will be for your business.

CHAPTER 6:

Predicting Financial Results

"What is talked about is a dream.
What is envisioned is exciting.
What is planned becomes possible.
What is scheduled is real."
– Tony Robbins

According to a study that was prepared by Clutch in 2019, 61% of small businesses didn't create a budget in 2018. As I mentioned earlier when we were preparing the vision for your business, how do you expect to realize financial success in your business if you don't clearly outline the pathway to getting there? Unfortunately, 61% of small businesses are missing the opportunity to provide clarity on their pathway to realizing the results they desire. And as of now, you can avoid being part of that statistic, and clearly understand how you realize real financial results.

How Much Do You Want to Make?

Let's begin by re-engineering the financial model. Instead of looking at the revenue, gross profit, and respective fixed costs associated with your business, let's start by defining the financial results you want to realize. In this sense, we want to define the bottom-line financial result you want to achieve in your business. For this, we will turn the financial model upside down and declare what you want the operating income to be. One item to consider would be whether or not to include wages and benefits costs for yourself (the owner). In theory, we would want to ensure that the entrepreneur is getting paid fair market value compensation in this exercise to ensure that, as the owner, you are not giving up a regular pay cheque at a normal job to put everything on the line as an entrepreneur and make less money.

To help you outline your financial goals, and to put them into a format that works best, I have created a document to get you started. This document follows the re-engineered financial results format discussed above, and can be found at gauvreaucpa.ca/the-wealthy-entrepreneur/resources. This document requires you to manually input some numbers, but also provides a pre-determined set of formulas that will help you calculate your overall targets. I have also included it as an example below. In this example, I started with the goal of generating $500,000 of operational income at the end of the year and included a $100,000 salary for the owner operator as fair market value compensation.

Outline the Fixed Costs

In this part of the exercise, you need to outline all the fixed costs that the company requires to operate on a day-to-day basis. As was discussed in the previous chapter, fixed costs are costs that do not change over the short-term, even if a business experiences changes in its sales volume or other activity levels.

Since fixed costs are relatively constant, the easiest way to determine what the fixed costs of the business are would be to review the most recent year's financial statements, or if your bookkeeping is up-to-date, review the most recent twelve-month trend in the business to identify what the annual fixed expenses will most likely be. In the example below, I have outlined a list of various fixed costs that are required to operate this business.

Gross Profit

As I previously mentioned, gross profit is the earnings a company makes after deducting the costs associated with making and selling its products, or the costs associated with providing its services. What we can determine is that once we know the results that we want to achieve (the operating income of the business), and we have completely outlined the fixed costs, according to how the calculation works, we are able to identify how much the company will need to realize in gross profit in order to deliver the desired results.

In our example, if the business wants to earn an operating income of $500,000, and the fixed costs of the business are $331,800, the company will need to generate a gross profit of $831,800 to realize that goal.

By understanding the gross profit necessary to achieve our goals, and once we understand what the gross profit margin is on our sales, we can determine the number of sales and the overall revenue that the company needs to realize to accomplish the financial goals.

Determining the Sales Mix

For many businesses, it is common to not just deliver one product or service, but to deliver multiple products or services. In this situation, many of the products or services that the company delivers are at different price points, and have different costs associated with delivering these products or services. One major weakness for many entrepreneurs is not having an understanding of the profitability and/or profit margin on each individual product or service that is delivered. This is problematic for the entrepreneur since some product or service lines may be very profitable and others may be losing money. Without having a handle on what area of your business is generating the most profit (or margin) on your sales, you cannot not fully understand what area of sales to focus on, and which ones will create the most profit for the business.

In an effort to assist you in understanding the profitability of each product or service you offer, I created a document that you can fill out that will analyze the different sources of revenue, their respective costs required to deliver the product or service, the overall volume of delivery for each of the individual items, and the individual and overall gross profit margin on the revenue. This is a very helpful document for looking at what areas you need to focus on growing in your business and can be used for scenario-based planning related to revenue growth. Not only will this document and exercise provide you with your overall profit margin on your sales mix, but it will also show you what areas of your business are the most profitable, and what areas you should focus on better promoting in the future. Obviously, the quantitative calculations of profitability on the sales mix are not the only considerations for the focus on future promotion and growth. As an entrepreneur, you must also consider the market risk associated with expanding in certain areas, the trends related

47

to demand for specified products or services, and the overall impact objectives of the organization, to ensure that your future growth is in alignment with the strategic vision of your business. Once you determine your sales mix on what products and/or services you are going to deliver, the document also calculates the overall gross profit margin of the business, which we require for predicting financial results. You can download this sales mix document at gauvreaucpa.ca/the-wealthy-entrepreneur/resources. Once this exercise is completed, you can input the overall gross profit margin for the sales mix, and you can then determine the sales required to deliver your desired operating income. In our example, once we input the profit margin of 60%, we have identified that we need to generate gross revenue of $1,386,333.33 in order to realize a net operating income in the business of $500,000.

Once you have determined your sales mix and the overall sales required for each product and/or service, you can determine the exact number of sales you need to make in each area of your business in order to realize your overall revenue and profitability target. This will be helpful once we review the overall accountability structure, define specific goals for each area of your business, and assign S.M.A.R.T. (specific, measurable, attainable, realistic, and timely) goals to each member of the team. We will address this next.

Operating income (or desired business profit)	500,000.00
FIXED COSTS	
Advertising	24,000.00
Bank charges and interest	12,000.00
Insurance	1,000.00
Interest	12,000.00
Management wages	100,000.00
Office and general	15,000.00
Professional development	24,000.00
Professional fees	10,000.00
Property tax	12,000.00
Repairs and maintenance	15Ê000,00
Rent	48,000.00
Telephone	1,800.00
Travel and entertainment	15,000.00
Utilities	12,000.00
Vehicle	30,000.00
Other	-
Total fixed costs	331,800.00
TOTAL REQUIRED GROSS PROFIT	831,800.00
Test (calculated gross profit (revenue minus variable costs))	831,800.00
TOTAL GROSS PROFIT PERCENTAGE	60%
VARIABLE COSTS	
Purchase of raw materials	375,000.00
Direct labor for assembly	146,500.00
Packaging	18,000.00
Wages and benefits (directly related to the product sale/delivery)	10,000.00

Supplies directly related to the delivery of the product	1,000.00
Shipping	1,000.00
Other direct sales costs (such as commissions, lead acquisition costs, etc.)	1,000.00
Vehicle costs (travel to deliver or sell the product)	1,500.00
Variable overhead costs	533,33
Total costs (NEED TO TOTAL THE BELOW PRE-DETERMINED TOTAL)	554,533.33
TOTAL CALCUALTED VARIABLE COSTS (PRE-DETERMINED)	554,533.33
Test (total inputted costs should equal pre-determined variable costs)	0,00
REVENUE	
Product revenue	1,386,333.33
Service revenue	-
Total costs (NEED TO TOTAL THE BELOW PRE-DETERMINED TOTAL)	1,386,333.33
TOTAL CALCULATED REVENUE (PRE-DETERMINED)	1,386,333.33

DETERMINING THE SALES MIX/GROSS PROFIT MARGIN	Product 1	Product 2	Product 3	Product 4	Product 5	Total
Sales Price	$500.00	$10,000.00	$650.00	$325.00	$99.00	N/A
Estimated number of units to be sold	800.00	14.00	465.00	400.00	4,183.00	-
VARIABLE COSTS						
Purchase of raw materials	135.00	3,000.00	150.00	75.00	-	-
Direct labor for assembly	50.00	500.00	50.00	25.00	-	-
Packaging	10.00	100.00	10.00	4.10	5.72	-
Wages and benefits (directly related to the product sale/delivery)	25.00	1,500.00	25.00	44.00	5.50	-
Supplies directly related to the delivery of the product	-	-	-	-	-	-
Shipping	10.00	-	-	-	-	-
Other direct sales costs (such as commissions, lead acquisition costs, etc.)	-	-	-	-	20.00	-
Vehicle costs (travel to delivery or sell the product)	-	-	-	-	-	-
Variable overhead costs	-	-	-	-	-	-
Total Sales	400,000.00	140,000.00	302,250.00	130,000.00	414,117.00	1,386,367.00
Total variable costs	184,000.00	71,400.00	109,275.00	59,240.00	130,593.26	554,508.26
Total gross profit	216,000.00	68,600.00	192,975.00	70,760.00	283,523.74	831,858.74
Total gross profit margin	54.00%	49.00%	63.85%	54.43%	68.46%	60.00%

CHAPTER 7

Outlining Key Outcomes

*"A good plan violently executed now is better
than a perfect plan executed next week."*
— George S. Patton

Now that you have outlined your goals and identified the required macro-level financial figures that you need to realize, you can start to bring those high-level goals back down to a real level, meaning figuring out what you need to accomplish today, this week, and this month that will drive results in your business so that you can achieve your long-term financial goals. However, before you start identifying these specific objectives, you need to understand how your organization works, and who is accountable for driving what results in your business.

Accountability Chart

In the simplest terms, every business is made up of three main components: marketing, operations, and finance. Let's look at each of these components in greater detail.

Marketing

This is the area of the business that is responsible for establishing relationships between the customers (or potential customers) and what the organization has to offer them. This may include:

1. Branding – the creation of the organization's logo, communication of the organization's values and purpose, how the organization is positioned in the market, and the perceived value of the products and/or services that are delivered to the market.

2. Advertising – the delivery of promotion and communication related to what the company offers to its customers and why they should buy it.

3. Communications – ongoing correspondence with customers and potential customers related to the products and/or services offered by the company, what the organization is developing for the future, and the messaging that establishes authority of the brand and demand for the products/services.

4. Sales – responsible for building relationships with individual clients, creating a direct link between those customers and what the company offers, identifying the needs and wants of the customers and providing them with a solution. At the end of the day, the sales element is responsible for making sales and delivering revenue for the business.

Operations

This is the business function that is responsible for the creation and delivery of goods and services. It involves planning and controlling all the resources needed to produce a company's goods and services as well as their delivery to the end user. Two specific areas that are the responsibility of the operations department (certainly with a crossover into marketing) would include customer relations and human resources.

1. Customer relations – This is the role within the organization that is responsible for providing customers with information about its products and/or services, helping manage customer expectations related to the delivery of the products and/or services, and maintaining the relationships between the clients and their delivery of products and/or services

2. Human resources – This is the role within the organization that is responsible for managing the human capital of the business, which includes recruiting and placing employees, managing their compensation and training, and managing long-term retention of the organization's employees.

Aside from overseeing the customer relations and human resources functions of the business, the major role of the operations department is to manage the resources and processes necessary to deliver the company's products and/or services. As you can see in the example accountability chart below, when there are multiple products and/or services that the company delivers, it may require multiple arms of the operations department to manage and facilitate their delivery. For as many products or services that the company offers, there should be a specific arm that deals directly with its delivery. We will discuss the reason for this as we continue to dive deeper below.

Finance

The finance area of the business is responsible for all financial aspects of the organization, including but not limited to the following:

1. Budgeting – this is the process of outlining the organization's financial goals and establishing expectation reports and financial benchmarking to predict what the financial results of the organization will be in the future, as well as ensuring that the organization's departments are being held accountable to eliminate unnecessary spending.

2. Reporting – this includes providing regular and ongoing financial reports to management so that they have the necessary financial information to make informed strategic decisions. In addition, they are responsible for financial reporting to the shareholders and any external parties such as financial lenders or government agencies.

3. Collections – this is the process of physically collecting funds from customers who have purchased products and/ or services. This could include collecting funds prior to or post-delivery of the product or service.

4. Payables – this is the management of bill payment, ensuring that appropriate cash is available to support payments, and optimizing the deferral of payments to best utilize the organization's financial resources.

5. Tax obligations – this is the process of managing tax filings, including business income and sales tax obligations, and managing the respective payments of these obligations.

6. Financing requirements – the goal of managing financing in a business is to ensure the company has the appropriate cash resources necessary to fulfill its obligations. Financing may include cash management, such as lines of credit to support inventory purchases, or may include financing for the purchase of capital additions such as businesses, equipment, and vehicles.

Who Is Responsible?

Now that we understand the overall organization accountability chart, we need to dive a little bit deeper and understand who is responsible for each element of the business. There are a few rules that need to be followed as we identify who is responsible.

1. One individual may be responsible for more than one area of the business, and that is okay. This will occur in many small organizations where there are limited team members. However, as an owner/operator, this is where we can identify areas for delegation. For example, the owner/manager may be responsible for marketing, finance, and operations; however, one team member is responsible for the delivery and result of product/service A, and another team member is responsible for the delivery and results of product/service B. As an organization continues to grow, it is imperative that we continue to push responsibility down to our team members. If we don't, we will begin to fail on delivering results to our customers.

2. There cannot be more than one individual responsible for any function. For example, related to Product/Service A, Joe and

Steve cannot be jointly responsible. Accountability becomes much more effective if each function of the business has a limited opportunity to blame others for the lack of positive results. Pick one individual who is responsible. This doesn't mean that there are not other contributors from the team, it just means that at the end of the day, one person is responsible for the overall outcome of that function.

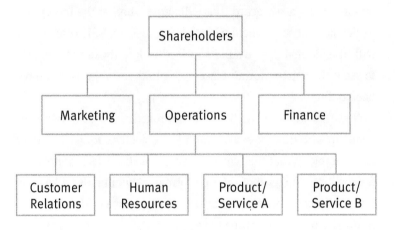

S.M.A.R.T. Objectives

Now that you have identified all the key functions of your business *and* you have determined who will ultimately be held responsible for that function, you are ready to dive deep and identify the goals of each function. When identifying the goals of each function, you should follow the S.M.A.R.T. methodology:

1. Specific – Well defined, clear, and fully understood
2. Measurable – The progress in attaining the goal can be identified and measured

3. Attainable – Possible to achieve
4. Realistic – It should be within reach and not an unrealisable objective
5. Timely – A deadline can be determined for when it needs to be achieved

The reason we want to follow the S.M.A.R.T. approach is so that we can create a scorecard that will show whether the individual responsible for each function is achieving their goals. This scorecard will provide real time results and feedback to those accountable to see if they are performing according to the standards that have been outlined.

Now that we have identified the approach, the goal would be to come up with three to seven S.M.A.R.T. objectives for each person accountable so that they can have very specific tasks that not only demonstrate the level of their performance but are also a key performance component to the overall performance of the company. In other words, these three to seven S.M.A.R.T. objectives should be tightly aligned with the organization's goals. By developing this scorecard for the organization and its key components, you will be able to identify the key performance indicators that will be driving the financial results of your business.

Let's look at an example of what these S.M.A.R.T. objectives look like in practice.

In Chapter 6 we looked at predicting the desired financial results for your business. In the example, the total revenue that the organization needed to generate was $1,386,333.33. We looked even further into what products the organization needed to deliver in order to generate those specific sales goals, and we came up with delivering five different products, with different sales prices, different associated direct costs, and different profitability. For our example here, let's look at a marketing objective for Product 1 and what some S.M.A.R.T. goals could be related to the marketing role.

1. Annual sales of 800 products at $500 per unit
   a. This would result in sixteen units being sold per week
   b. Weekly revenue of $8,500

As you can see with the above, sixteen units per week is specific, we can measure it by reviewing the number of sales for this particular product during the week, it appears attainable (just over three sales per day on average), it appears realistic, and we can put an end date of a weekly goal, which makes it very timely. The result here, related to the marketing objective for Product 1, is that we can certainly tell if the marketing group has done their job in hitting their targets. We can then put this on a scoreboard and keep track of the progress. If the marketing group accomplishes this goal, the organization will be well on its way to realizing its financial targets.

Let's try another one.

2. Assuming your closing rate is 20%, you would need to generate 4,000 phone calls and/or meetings related to Product 1 during the year to sell 800 products
   a. This would result in seventy-seven phone calls per week
   b. Maintain a closing rate of > 20%

In this situation, the marketing group will need to generate sufficient leads to ensure that enough calls are booked so that the business can meet its sales target. This would mean seventy-seven phone calls per week, and a closing rate of greater than 20%. Hitting these targets would guarantee that the sixteen units get sold per week. Under this objective, we are diving deeper into our goal to find key attributes that are driving our sales targets. This objective is specific, it is measurable (either through a CRM program or manual tracking), is attainable (assuming there is a team of two or more people – one call per hour each), it appears realistic, and has a set timeline for a weekly goal.

The above examples should start to demonstrate how you can create short-term S.M.A.R.T goals across your organization so that each area of the business is aligned to delivering the overall financial objectives of the business. The goal for these objectives is to ensure that everyone on your team has a report card that provides them with direct feedback related to their performance, and that their performance is aligned with the company objectives.

I would encourage each accountability area (customer relations, human resources, Product 1, etc.) to meet with those who work in that department and provide each of the team members with three to seven S.M.A.R.T. goals as well. That way each individual on the team is driving the results of the department, which is driving results for the business.

See Fig. 7 on page 61.

Review Process

Once these S.M.A.R.T. objectives are in place, you are ready to begin. I recommend that you have a weekly leadership meeting where you bring in the scorecard and have an accountability session, going through each of the objectives and assessing whether or not individual members of the team are delivering the results the business needs.

The meeting should look something like the following:

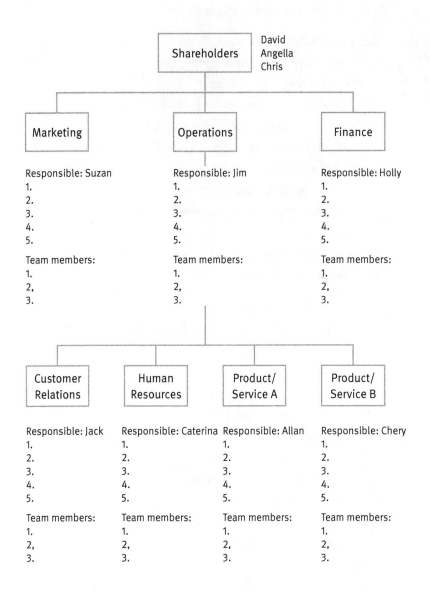

Fig. 7

Weekly leadership meeting agenda (60 minutes)

1. Agenda review (5 minutes)
2. Prior week follow-up items (5 minutes)
3. Scorecard review (10 minutes)
4. Any objectives not met get added to a follow-up list
5. Follow up – discuss reasons for not hitting objectives, what needs to change, what support/resources everyone needs to hit next week's objectives (10 minutes)
6. Other issues, problems, or opportunities (15 minutes)
7. New clients, client announcements, employee recognitions (5 minutes)
8. Items to follow up on for next week (5 minutes)
9. Conclude (5 minutes)

By implementing this weekly leadership meeting into your business, you will consistently stay on top of the progress your team is making on achieving the goals of the business. This will ensure that everyone is completely aligned with the goals of the organization, and it will create a culture of engagement and performance that your business has never seen before. The goal here would be to schedule this meeting on a weekly basis, with everyone required to be present, and no absences (unless due to illness or vacation).

We will address the implementation of the weekly leadership meeting into a regular schedule of success as we get into Chapter 9, which is related to staying accountable to your goals. First, we need to discuss the necessity of creating a financial scoreboard in your business.

CHAPTER 8:

Creating a Scoreboard

"If you can't read the scoreboard, you don't know the score. If you don't know the score, you can't tell the winners from the losers."
– Warren Buffett

Let's set the scene here. You are heading to watch your favourite team play basketball in the big city. On your way, you get stuck in traffic, which puts you late for tip off, and even worse, you end up getting to the venue forty-five minutes late. It is a big game, so you don't want to miss a thing. When you arrive at the stadium, you rush in to see tens of thousands of people there cheering for the home team. You rush to your seats to see that the scoreboard isn't working ... what is happening? You continue to watch the action; your team is taking shots from all over the court, but you can't particularly tell if they are making two-point shots or if they are three-point shots. At the same time, the opposing team seems to be making similar shots, so it looks pretty even. You are frustrated because you don't really know what is going on. The excitement is high, but you have no idea what the score is, no idea what quarter the game is in, if your favourite team is winning, or how much time is left in the game for your team to bring home the win.

Now, let's picture this in a different light. When you arrive to the game forty-five minutes late, you realize it is the fourth quarter with five minutes to spare. Although the game has been back and forth, at the beginning of the game your team appears to have dominated. The score is ninety-two to fifty-four. You are very satisfied that your team is winning, and you join in the celebration. It is very clear that your team is tracking to win the game and is well positioned to do so easily. Thank goodness that you could see exactly where the game was at, so that you could enjoy watching your team succeed.

Which approach sounds better? In the first situation, you go into the game blind, no idea how the team has performed in the past. You can't really tell how they are doing now, and you don't have any certainty if they are on track to win. Or in the second, when you arrive at the game, you can see exactly how the team is doing. You can see that there are only a few minutes left for your team to achieve the goal: winning the game.

The scoreboard provides a significant amount of clarity around the game and provides you with an up-to-date report on what is being accomplished and provides the team with an update on whether they need to change their strategy mid-game to accomplish the end goals.

Now think about your business. Do you feel like you have clarity around how your team is performing, how your business is doing financially, and if you are on target to accomplish your financial objectives? If you don't know what the score is inside your business, how do you know if you are making money? How do you know if you are going to accomplish your financial goals? How do you know if you are making the right decisions daily to maximize the financial performance of your business so that you can continue to have the biggest impact in your business? So many entrepreneurs are working hard to accomplish their goals but neglect the implementation of a scoreboard, which will provide them reassurance that their hard work is making them progress toward their goals. Let's take the first step toward creating financial clarity.

How to Create a Financial Scoreboard

Having an up-to-date financial scoreboard for your business is essential. Not only does it provide better information to facilitate making effective financial decisions, but it also helps to realize financial success in your business. As technology continues to advance and artificial intelligence and cloud-based solutions become more sophisticated, it is becoming easier to find a solution that fits with your organization and is easy to implement to make your financial scoreboard a reality.

Find the Right Solution

As I previously mentioned, there appear to be endless solutions available to help you keep your financial records up-to-date in a simple and real time fashion. The following are some of the solutions that we see on a regular basis:

- QuickBooks Online
- Xero
- Sage 50
- Freshbooks
- Zoho
- Wave
- And many more

Although you could spend hours reviewing the numerous solutions available, the important part of finding the solution is choosing one and implementing it. At the end of the day, most of these platforms offer a very similar solution, only with a different look. If you have specific needs such as job costing, manufacturing, or inventory management, you may want to review these specific areas of the software to ensure they will meet your needs. If you have no complicated and specific tracking requirements in your business, then any one of these solutions will work for you. With that in mind, the product that we see most frequently and that is easy to use and provides good financial reporting options is QuickBooks Online. QuickBooks Online is the most popular solution on the market, and they continue to invest significantly in improving the user experience.

Connect Your Accounts

Once you have chosen your desired solution, it is time to get it connected. One of the many features related to the many cloud-based accounting solutions is that they can tie directly into your bank feed, which allows for the bookkeeping software to pull the transactions that are taking place inside your bank and credit card accounts and pull them into your system on a live basis. This provides for the opportunity to reconcile your transactions as you go. Not only does this allow you to have up-to-date financial records, but it will simplify the data entry process of your bookkeeping department.

Stay on Top of It

Regardless of the solution that you choose, it is essential that you keep your financial information up-to-date. And here's the best part: if the idea of keeping up with your financial bookkeeping tasks is causing anxiety in your life, and you feel like you have higher priority items to be spending your time on, that is fine ... outsource it! I have an inside scoop on this one: my team at www.GauvreauCPA.ca can have this taken care of for you. At the end of the day, if you can't keep up, make sure you bring someone in who can. The cost to outsource your bookkeeping is minimal compared to the value you receive in exchange, which is more time to focus on what is driving your business, as well as having accurate and timely financial reports that are essential for making informed strategic decisions and that will allow you to see how your business is performing right now.

Take It to the Next Level

At this point we have provided you with the relevant information and resources to ensure you have up-to-date financial information, which is essential to ensuring your business is performing well financially. Now we want to take your financial scoreboard to the next level. This involves having the information we created in Chapter 6 added to your financial scoreboard. As we discussed in Chapter 6, having forecasted financial information allows the business to see what its financial goals and benchmarks for financially succeeding are, and by introducing these figures into your scoreboard, we will have a financial benchmark to compare the current results to confirm that we are on track to realizing our goals.

Creating the financial scoreboard brings future goals and current reality together, making for a very powerful and informative financial picture of your business. Creating budgeted financial expectations is one of the most important factors to creating financial success in any business. This is because it outlines the goals of your business and provides you with a framework to work within that will establish a benchmark for the results you need to generate in order to reach your goals. However, if you don't track your actual progress to your budgeted figures, you are really missing out on the opportunity to see if you are on track to achieving these goals. When combined, expectations and reality provide valuable information that demonstrates how you are progressing with your financial goals and allows you the opportunity to make changes in your business along the way to either get back on track, or to adjust your expectations back to a new reality. Having this information available on demand allows you to manage expectations and eliminate any financial surprises that would traditionally occur at the end of the year when you review your results.

CHAPTER 9:

Staying Accountable

*"Unless commitment is made, there are
only promises and hopes; but no plans."*
— Peter F. Drucker

We are at the stage in our framework where the majority of the planning process has been completed, and we move into the execution phase. You have outlined your goals, you have determined the financial model of success for your business, you have determined what the key financial metrics are that will drive results in your business, and you have created a financial scoreboard to measure the ongoing performance of your business. Now it is time to deliver results.

The key to delivering extraordinary results in your business is to stay scheduled, ensure you stay on track, and revise your goals and individual objectives along the way. There are two elements that you will need to track: your goal scorecard and your financial scoreboard. With that in mind, I have outlined a schedule that will keep your team on track and will help you stay accountable to each other throughout the process.

Schedule of Success

Daily Huddle

Depending on the size of your team, the way you will schedule your daily huddle may differ. A daily huddle consists of putting fifteen minutes aside to meet with your team to discuss the following:

1. **What did you say you were going to do yesterday, and did you do it?**

   This is an opportunity for the individuals within your team to discuss what they vocalized as their goals for the day prior. The goal with discussing what you said you were going to do, and the reality of whether you did it, is a major accountability opportunity for the team. If you consistently don't hit your goals, then you need to review the goals set, whether they are realistic, and whether you are making a sufficient contribution to the team goals.

   This is also an opportunity for the team, and specifically the leadership team, to monitor the workflow to ensure that sufficient delivery is taking place for the organization to realize its goals. The intent for this process is that it is a quick update to ensure everyone is on the same page, to ensure that there are no ongoing problems or issues with the deliverables, and to hold each other accountable to what was committed to being complete.

   This should be a quick process, with each team member contributing their piece in under twenty seconds. If all is good, you then move on to the next team member.

2. What are you going to accomplish today?

This is an opportunity to hear from the team what tasks they are going to complete by the day's end. It is also an opportunity to hear from team members what they feel is a reasonable task list to be completed. By announcing to their colleagues what they intend on completing that day, you are creating an accountability process that will deliver high performance habits for your team. At the end of the day, each employee will want to ensure that they are contributing to the overall team objectives, and they really don't want to come back to the team tomorrow to say they didn't complete what they said they would.

Again, this is intended to occur quickly. Each team member should be able to state what they are going to contribute and accomplish within twenty seconds.

3. What are you stuck on? And where do you need help?

This is an area where each team member can ask for help. Specifically, if there is something that has constrained one of the team members from delivering on one of their projects, they can ask for help.

One idea of where a team member is stuck would be if they are missing information and need someone to obtain the missing documentation. It may very well be the case that one member of the leadership team or other direct client connection may have the information that is missing already, and that it just hadn't been transitioned to the appropriate team member. Since there is constant communication, any missed information will be caught early and will avoid any delays in delivering the product or service. When it is identified that a team member is stuck or missing some information relevant to completing their job, this may be an area for the leadership team to offer support and mentorship to individual team members based on areas of complexities in their tasks at hand. Showing this support daily will reinforce the fact that everyone is working together to accomplish results. It will also show the entire team that leadership is in place to support each employee to complete their daily tasks and hit their targets.

Depending on the number of team members who are stuck or need help, this process could be quick, or may take a few minutes. This is a great opportunity to demonstrate the leadership support of the team members and encourage the collaboration of members to deliver high performance results to the clients and drive results for the business.

4. Announcements

This is an opportunity to share positive events happening in the business, and for individuals to share great news around their personal lives and accomplishments. This only takes a brief moment, but allows for the team to unite around the excitement of the business opportunities for the future, and provides a vehicle to share support and encouragement for things happening in the lives of the team that happen outside of the office.

The huddle meeting should have a designated individual who is responsible for getting it started and ensuring everyone is there on time. Ideally, it would be run by one individual team member who has a responsibility with the oversight of the operations of the business. In addition, it would be someone who is organized, is punctual, and is willing to lead the session. The goal is to keep everyone on track and ensure the meeting takes place as efficiently as possible. If there are specific concerns related to the progress of any individual team member, if you feel that they may be stuck or are spinning their wheels on their current tasks, or if you feel that their prioritization of tasks needs to be addressed, it is essential that you connect with them individually to see what support they need or to provide them with any additional direction they may need related to the expectations of their delivery and job performance.

Weekly Leadership Meeting

The idea of the weekly leadership team meeting was introduced in Chapter 7. The goal of the weekly leadership team meeting is to ensure that the three to seven objectives that each leader is responsible for are being delivered, are on track, and if there are any ongoing issues or reasons that deliverables are not being met, that they are addressed early, and that the appropriate support is provided. The weekly leadership meeting should include any leadership member who is directly responsible for the delivery of the marketing, finance, or operational performance of the business. This would include any leadership team members who are responsible for delivering operational divisions within the operations department. Let's look at the weekly leadership meeting in more detail below.

Weekly Leadership Meeting Agenda (60 minutes)

1. **Agenda Review (5 minutes)**
   The agenda review is for quickly going through the eight steps on the list, to ensure that these are appropriate for the weekly

73

agenda, and to add any pressing items to Step 6 at the start of the meeting. For example, if there is an employee issue where there needs to be a termination, we can add that item (and any others that leaders are prepared to speak to) on the agenda prior to starting the scoreboard review.

2. Prior Week Follow-Up Items (5 minutes)

At the end of each meeting, there will be follow-up items identified during Step 7. In this five-minute period, review any necessary follow-up from the previous week's meeting. For example, in the previous week your marketing department was starting a new campaign that was to launch mid-week; however, there was a delay and your team wanted some follow-up. At this point in the meeting, we will discuss this and any other unresolved issues that were carried forward.

3. Scorecard Review (10 minutes)

The goal of the scorecard review is to review each leader's three to seven S.M.A.R.T. goals/objectives that were identified during the scorecard creation, and determine whether the objectives have been met, are on track, or if there are any issues related to their delivery.

Below is an example of a simple scorecard for the marketing department. As you can see, most of the objectives have been completed, however, there appears to be an issue with objective number five. It is obvious from this scorecard that something needs to be done to ensure that this objective does not cause a problem in delivering on the objectives of the business. This will be discussed in the next portion of the meeting.

Company Scorecard
Weekly Leadership Meeting
Marketing

Objective	Week 1	Week 2	Week 3	Week4	Week5
1		▓			
2			▓		
3	▓				
4					
5	▓	▓	▓		
6					
7					

4. Follow Up on Scoreboard Results (10 minutes)

Now that we have pinpointed the goals that have been met, and those that haven't, you need to discuss the specific reasons for not hitting objectives, what needs to change before next week's meeting, and what support and/or resources everyone needs to hit next week's objectives.

In reviewing these objectives, it is also a great opportunity for the team to collaborate and problem solve how one area may be struggling and how the team can best support the completion of the objectives.

Now that any issues have been addressed and the team has collaborated to determine the best action necessary to address any missed targets, the meeting leader will add the missed objective to a follow-up list to ensure that any issues from week to week are addressed and remedied.

This is the primary goal of the leadership team meeting, to ensure that the entire team stays aligned to the company objectives, stays accountable to the goals that have been outlined, and that any issues with delivery are identified early so that adjustments can be made, and the overall goals of the organization can be met.

5. **Other Issues, Problems, or Opportunities (15 minutes)**
Once the scoreboard results and plan of action have been addressed, we now move on to any other issues, problems, or opportunities that need to be addressed. All of these items should have been added at the start of the meeting or may have come up as you have moved through your scoreboard analysis. This would include any employee or staffing issues, actions of competitors, client complaints, product or service delivery issues, or could look at potential opportunities that are available such as business acquisitions, strategic partnerships, speaking engagements, networking events, etc.

This is a very important area of the weekly meeting to ensure that any issues or opportunities within the business are identified, discussed, and resolved. Again, this keeps the leadership team aligned in your goals, and unites the message for the entire organization.

6. **New Clients, Client Announcements, Employee Recognitions (5 minutes)**
This is a great opportunity to share new opportunities that have arisen or progress on a new initiative that has been happening in the business, and for the leadership team to share insights about employee contributions, personal and team accomplishments, and recognize the contributions of individual team members. This is an opportunity for the leadership team to unite around the excitement about the business opportunities for the future and provides a vehicle

to share support and encouragement for things happening in the lives of the team that happen outside of the office.

7. **Items to Follow up on for Next Week (5 minutes)**
This is a brief recap of the items that are on the list to be followed up on, who is responsible, the anticipated result, and the expectation that each item will be identified at the start of the next meeting prior to reviewing the next week's results.

8. **Conclude (5 minutes)**
Conclude the meeting with a quick recap of the items that have been accomplished in the last week, the opportunities that await, and any company accomplishments that were identified earlier.

As was the case with the daily huddle, the weekly leadership meeting should have a designated individual who is responsible for getting it started and ensuring everyone is there on time. Ideally, it would be run by one individual team member who has a responsibility with the oversight of the operations of the business. In addition, it would be someone who is organized, is punctual, and is willing to lead the session. If it is not the individual who is responsible for the operations of the business, it should be that person who is responsible for appointing a member of the team to lead these meetings. The goal is to keep everyone on track and ensure the meeting takes place as efficiently as possible.

Monthly Financial Review

You have now set up your daily huddle and weekly leadership meeting. You can see that individuals on your team are now being held accountable to their tasks, and the team is aligned and performing at a high level. The next step is ensuring that the performance of your team is converting into financial results for the business. You need to do this on a regular (monthly) basis to ensure that if the objectives are not converting into financial results, you catch them quickly, adjust, and keep the business heading in the right financial direction. If these reviews do not take place regularly, you could miss out on the opportunity to correct any issues until it is too late, and profits could be lost. Let's set this up now.

Financial Dashboard – Budget vs. Actual Review (month- and year-to-date)

As you will remember back in Chapter 6, we outlined the financial expectations of the business. This involved creating a budgeted income statement for the year, from which we designed key goals/objectives for business leaders to ensure that what was required to be delivered was being done. The first report that we want to review is the budget vs. actual results of the business. This will take the expected results and compare it to what occurred. The wonderful part about financial results is that they don't lie. The actual results don't have any excuses, don't have any bias, and do not cater to the interests of any particular department. Just like the scorecard, the financial dashboard will demonstrate whether you are achieving your goals or not.

Thinking back to the discussion of your financial model, there are a few areas that you should focus on:

1. Revenue – Did your company generate the sales necessary to hit the overall revenue targets of the organization? If it did, why did it? If it did not, why did it not?

2. Gross profit – Although your business may or may not have achieved its revenue targets, it is even more important that it generated the gross profit expected in order to cover the fixed costs and drive the profitability of the business. Again, if you hit the gross profit target, why so? If you did not, why not?

3. Gross margin – When we initially discussed the financial model, we reviewed the profit margin derived on each sale that you made, understanding that as sales go up, so too do your direct costs. You want to review your gross margin to ensure that you have maintained your desired profit per unit of sale, and to ensure that there have not been any unexpected costs that have been incurred, that your cost per unit hasn't increased, and that you are on track to generating your expected profit per unit of sale. Did you hit your gross margin per unit? If yes, great. If not, why?

4. Fixed cost review – It was discussed earlier that fixed costs stay relatively unchanged from month to month. The goal with reviewing the fixed costs would be to ensure that they are in line with the budgeted figures. Any areas that are above or below budgeted figures should be reviewed, and any variance should be addressed. You should be looking to see if any fixed costs had unexpectedly increased, if any essential investments (such as marketing) have been neglected, and if there has been a pattern of excessive spending that needs to be reviewed.

5. Cash flow – Even though your business may be profitable, it is very important to review how your business cash flow is performing. In Chapter 12, we will dive deeper into how

to improve the cash flow of your business, but on a monthly basis you should be converting your profit into how the cash flowed in or out. Below is an example on how to set this up so that you can see if your company cash flow is performing as expected.

Company Cash Flow Analysis
Monthly

Net income (from actual results)	$ XXX,XXX
Additions to cash:	
Amortization/depreciation	$ XXX,XXX
Decrease in accounts receivable	$ XXX,XXX
Decrease in inventory	$ XXX,XXX
Increase in accounts payable	$ XXX,XXX
Increase in taxes payable	$ XXX,XXX
Financing received	$ XXX,XXX
	$ XXX,XXX
Subtractions from cash	
Increase in accounts receivable	$ XXX,XXX
Increase in inventory	$ XXX,XXX
Decrease in accounts payable	$ XXX,XXX
Decrease taxes payable	$ XXX,XXX
Asset purchases	$ XXX,XXX
Debt repayment	$ XXX,XXX
Shareholder payments	$ XXX,XXX
	$ XXX,XXX

It is important that when reviewing the financial analysis identified above that you review these on a monthly basis and on a year-to-date basis. When you review the monthly report, you may see results that suggest that you are slightly behind on some of your financial targets; however, if you have been slightly behind your targets for six months straight, it may lead to a larger year-to-date deficiency to your goals that may be a problem that needs to be addressed.

At the end of the meeting, you should have answers to all the following questions:

1. Have we hit our budgeted targeted revenue and gross profit?
2. Are our fixed expenses aligned with our projected figures?
3. How is our cash management performing? Do we have sufficient cash or cash resources to carry on business? Do we need to investigate any financial instruments to assist (such as a line of credit)?
4. Are we overspending?
5. Are we profitable?
6. Are we on track to realizing our annual financial goals?

This meeting should be run by the financial leader of the business (or by a qualified financial expert outside your business). It is imperative that the person running the meeting has the necessary qualifications, expertise, and experience to properly analyze and interpret the financial information. In addition, it should include any of the relevant leadership team that can influence the financial results of the business or who would have knowledge of what results should be anticipated, so that they can question any unexpected discrepancies.

Reviewing the financial figures on a monthly basis will provide you with clarity on how the business is performing and will provide you with reassurance that the business is heading in the right direction to realize extraordinary financial results. It will also provide you with the facts of how your business is performing, and if it is not performing up to your expectations, you can take quick action to change the outcome. If you don't review these figures, you may be assuming that everything is going to plan and may have a surprise at the end of the year that everything is off track. The goal is to ensure that your scoreboard is up-to-date and that you review it on a monthly basis to provide feedback on your progress.

Quarterly Goal/Accountability Review

The quarterly leadership team update is a day that you can dedicate to getting off-site with your leadership team to review the past quarter's results, to see where the company is heading, and to realign the team with the overall company objectives. I suggest off-site as a good option for the meeting as it is away from constant distractions such as phone calls, emails, and individual interruptions.

The quarterly off-site meeting should look something like this:

1. **CEO/Partner Update**

    The goal of the CEO/partner update is to share a voice from the top of the organization, recognizing how the company has progressed, where it is heading, recognizing contributions from the leadership team, and looking into the future vision for the business. This will set the tone for the day and will share enthusiasm for the goals of the organization.

2. **Financial Results**

    When we originally set out the vision of your business in Chapter 4, we set up the expectations for the business to realize certain benchmarks over ten years, three years, and twelve months. Since we have been reviewing the financial results of the business on a monthly basis, everyone should be aware of where the company stands financially. However, when you review the financial results for the quarter, you should tie the results back into the three-year and ten-year goals and determine if these are still reasonable based on the most recent performance of the business.

As a secondary task related to the financial review, you can tie in the overall financial results to the individual performance of the accountability centers, identifying areas of the business where increased results need to occur in order for the ten-year targets to be realized. This will be a nice lead-in to your departmental presentations and the revision of the scorecard/objectives.

3. **Strategy session – Future Outlook of the Business**
   Every quarter, it is important to review the goals of the business, and to ensure that its strategy aligns with its goals. A few items to consider with having a strategic review would be as follows:
   o Human Capital Evaluation – Do you have the right people in the right seats, and do you have sufficient resources to deliver what you need to?
   o Marketing – Is your overall marketing and branding relaying the message that you need it to?
   o Client Experience – How is the client experience performing? What do you need to do to improve the client journey with your organization?
   o Company Values – Are the employees aligned with the values of the business? Have the values changed?

o Strategic Position – Where are you positioned inside your market? Is competition creating new pressures? And do you need to adjust your positioning in the market?

4. **Departmental Presentations**

This is an opportunity for each accountability center to present how their department has been performing and a means of reviewing:

o What resources are some of the constraints of the department? And what is needed to continue to grow and succeed?

o What opportunities does each department have to improve? To add additional value to customers and to the organization?

o What are the strengths of the department? And how can each department help other elements of the business succeed?

5. **Scorecard Revision**

This would be reviewing the three to seven core objectives of each accountability center, and modifying them if necessary, as the company evolves, increases its volume, and expected results change. You should review every single objective and see if anything needs to be modified going forward. The goal here would be to realign the objectives with the goals of the organization. For example, if the sales are continuing to increase, the number of leads required will need to increase to ensure sufficient demand is being created to hit sales targets. Once completed, the updated scorecard numbers will be implemented in the next weekly leadership meeting.

6. Conclusion

Conclude the meeting with a recap of where the company has been, the opportunities for the future, and the revised scorecard and responsibilities of each leadership member to drive results for the company. End with a clear path to executing the company objectives and delivering extraordinary financial results.

Quarterly Relay Meeting

The relay meeting is a meeting that happens within a few days after the quarterly goal/accountability review session. This is a summarized presentation of the quarterly goal/accountability review and is presented by the leadership group as a means of informing the entire team how the business is performing, where you are going, and updating the three to seven objectives of each accountability center. The purpose is to align the entire team with the updated goals of the organization and ensure everyone is on the same page to deliver extraordinary financial results for the business. This meeting should include everyone in the organization as an opportunity to clearly communicate the past success, the future direction, and how their role is essential in the future success of the organization.

CHAPTER 10:

Growing Your Business

"If you are not growing, you are dying."
— Tony Robbins

When I started my own business back in 2008, I was committed to creating something incredible. I had a very clear vision of where I wanted to go and what I wanted to accomplish. Along the way I have hired consultants and business coaches to help guide me, provide me with invaluable advice, and support me in achieving goals I wouldn't otherwise have been able to accomplish. These investments and relationships have opened many doors and continue to provide extraordinary opportunities as I continue to invest in these relationships. As I mentioned previously, one of the most unique opportunities that came out of working with a coach from Australia came back in 2015 when I was introduced to Tony Robbins. I remember the connection being made, and remember Tony calling my office to ask me if I would be interested in becoming one of his partners in the Global Accounting Advisors group. This was a group of hand-picked business advisors, CPAs, and tax experts who he wanted to work with his clients who attended his business mastery event. Of course, I was more than intrigued. I remember attending my first business mastery event, joining over 2,000 attendees, watching in awe as Tony rocked the stage and brought so much value to attendees. It was a life changing experience, that's for sure. And, you guessed it, I jumped into the opportunity to join Tony and his global experts in the Global Accounting Advisors group.

One of the benefits to joining Tony over the years and attending numerous business mastery events was learning from his network of industry experts and business gurus. One of the best in the business is Jay Abraham. Jay has been identified as one of the top five executive coaches in the US (according to *Forbes*) and is well known for being one of the greatest marketing minds in the world.

When I first met Jay at one of the business master events, I was introduced to the concept of business growth and "Jay Abraham's the only three ways to grow a business" concept. This is one of the most valuable yet simple concepts I have ever learned, and I want to share this with you now.

Jay Abraham's "The Only Three Ways to Grow a Business"

1. Increase the number of customers
2. Increase the average transaction value
3. Increase the frequency of repurchase

Let's look at each of the three ways in a little bit greater detail.

1. Increase the number of customers

This is the most traditional concept of growing a business, which is exactly like it suggests: just adding new customers to your business.

The idea here is that you will add customers, and you will lose customers, so it would be the net increase in customers that you need to focus on. This just makes good sense. If you have more customers who are buying from you, you will increase your revenue.

Here are some suggestions as to how you could increase your number of customers:

- Increase retention of existing customers – this would require less new client acquisition as the "net new customer" number would have to be less if you are retaining everyone.

- Purchase a new client list or business – by purchasing a new client list, you will make a significant jump in revenue.

- Organic client acquisition – this is the direct result of increasing your lead generation and converting those prospects into clients (lead generation x conversion rate = acquired clients). Again, this is the more traditional approach, so let me dive a bit deeper and provide some ideas as to creating leads and improving your conversion rate.

Lead Generation

Lead generation is the process of identifying and cultivating prospective customers for a business's products or services. In essence, you are looking to marketing strategies to increase interest in your product or services so that you can convert interested parties into buyers.

Here are a few ways to generate leads in your business:

- Create an active YouTube channel and followers
- Advertisements

- Creating articles
- Blog posts
- Physical brochures
- Signage (building signs, billboards, vehicle wraps, etc.)
- Direct mail
- Email marketing
- Facebook
- Google Ads and AdWords
- Instagram
- Links on third party websites
- Newspaper
- Media releases
- PR campaigns
- Radio
- TV ads
- Referrals
- Search engine optimization
- LinkedIn
- Speaking engagements
- Sponsorship
- Telemarking
- Testimonials
- Twitter
- Webinars
- Website

The above are all valid lead generation strategies (with many more available). The key is finding the platform (or multiple platforms) that are most effective for you and your business, are cost effective, and produce the best leads for your dollar spent.

Client Conversion

Client conversion is the process of turning prospects into paying customers. The higher the conversion rate, the more clients you generate. If you were looking to acquire a set number of new customers, if your conversion rate is higher, the cost associated with lead generation will be lower. Although conversion is equally important, much of the focus is pointed in the direction of lead generation. Let's identify some ways that you can improve your client conversion rate:

- Accept all payment types (don't just accept cash)
- Clearly articulate your value proposition
- Deliver remarkable service
- Be available
- Tighten up your sales process (find what works best and do that)
- Complete sales training – proven techniques

When looking at increasing the number of customers, the quickest way to get there is through acquisition. This is why so many large organizations have a very clearly defined acquisition strategy. Alternatively, the slower way to grow your customers is through lead generation and client conversion. It is certainly much less expensive to follow the latter; however, it takes time to refine your process to ensure you are getting effective and efficient results.

2. Increase the Average Transaction Value

This is often the most overlooked approach to revenue growth: the dreaded price increase. Although it is often overlooked, it is the simplest and most immediate way to create revenue growth inside your business. In working with over five hundred entrepreneurs across the world, one area that our team at Gauvreau CPA continues to review during the strategic growth process is the pricing strategy. There is a large stigma attached to pricing sensitivity with many entrepreneurs. What I can tell you is that, even in a competitive market, if you are offering value with what you sell, pricing is more of a sensitive issue with the entrepreneur than it is with the customer. I have an example for you. I work with a client who sells coffee (amongst other products and services). As you can imagine, coffee is a pretty generic product that can be purchased on almost every street corner. However, the particular client I worked with had a very unique space where environment and service were far superior to any other location. The business was looking for a way to increase their revenue, and I offered the suggestion of a price increase. As you can imagine (as you are thinking to yourself right now), the business owner suggested that her clients were too sensitive to introduce a price increase. In fact, she thought that any sort of price increase would price her coffee sales right out of the market. In trusting my guidance and persistence with wanting to make positive change for her business, she introduced a 10% price increase (again, the 10% was my suggestion – she thought it was way too much). At the end of the day, when the pricing increase was implemented, no customers even identified it as a concern. Shocker, right? It happens all the time! Clients are not as sensitive to a price increase as we entrepreneurs are. The business owner was so thrilled with the results, that she introduced a 10% price increase across the board on all of her other products and services. The result: hundreds of thousands of dollars added to her bottom-line. Even better, she has a scheduled strategic price increase that will occur semi-annually from here on in, which will continue to drive improved profitability and bottom-line income into her business for the foreseeable future.

91

Here would be my advice to you. If you have a product or service that is in high demand, and you seem too busy to deal with all of the chaos of running the business and delivering to the many customers, but you have a unique value proposition (or you offer more value in service or premium product as compared to your competition), you should consider a price increase. Worst case scenario, you lose a few customers, but you better serve those you value. The result will be increased revenue and increased profitability in your business.

3. Increase the Frequency of Repurchase

The idea related to the frequency of repurchase is that if you have a set number of customers, who only buy a particular product once during the year, how do you get them to buy that product twice per year, or how do you induce them into a new product purchase in addition to what they are already buying? Some examples of increasing the frequency of purchase would be:

- Offering additional products at discounted pricing when the purchase takes place
- Create a customer nurturing strategy that, once they make an initial purchase, an automated email sequence or social media advertisement will offer them complimentary or additional purchase options on a consistent and regular basis
- Introduce new products or services
- Upsell customers into a package that includes multiple products
- Create an extraordinary experience
- Ask for referrals (a referral could count toward new customers or could be an increase in the frequency of repurchase)

- Introduce the customer to another department within the business to see if they need any additional products or services

At the end of the day, as Jay Abraham simply states, there are only three ways to grow a business. However, the simplification of this concept is not the most exciting part. If you can determine a way to have your business increase all three areas at the same time, the results turn into exponential growth. Let me show you what I mean.

The formula works like this:

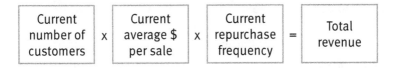

So, let's say that you feel comfortable committing to increasing each of the three areas by 10% during the next year. Meaning, you are going to acquire 10% more new customers, increase the average sale price by 10%, and you are going to increase the frequency of purchase by 10%. Here are the results:

Now, let's see what happens with a 20% growth in all areas:

Exponential growth. Pretty amazing results, right? Now, let's look at mixing it up a bit. Let's look at how we increase the revenue in our business by 150%:

Increase 33%	X	Increase 25%	X	Increase 50%	=	Increase by 150%

Isn't this amazing?! I can sense that most people may doubt the math on this, unless we use a specific example, so here we go:

1,000 customers	X	Average price of $500	X	Purchase 5 times per year	=	$2,500,000
Increase to 1,200 customers	X	Average price increase to $500	X	Increase to 6 times per year	=	$4,320,000

As you can see from the above, by introducing a 20% increase in customers, a 20% increase in the average transaction value, and a 20% increase in the frequency of repurchase, the business would increase from $2,500,000 in revenue to $4,320,000, which is an increase of 72.8%.

The purpose of sharing these examples is to demonstrate the simplicity in establishing a strategy around business growth. In addition, if you are able to increase multiple areas of your business, your business will not just grow, it will grow at an exponential rate.

CHAPTER 11:

Profit Maximization

"Rule No. 1: Never lose money. Rule
No. 2: Never forget rule No.1."
– Warren Buffett

To be part of a growing business can be exciting, not to mention that as you continue to grow, you have the opportunity to contribute and deliver more of your value offering to more people. However, just because you are growing, doesn't mean that you are making a profit. The purpose of this chapter will be to understand how you can maximize your business profitability to ensure the future sustainability of your business, to save the resources necessary to reinvest in future growth, and to allow for reasonable compensation for the shareholders.

One item we need to ensure we are clear on as we enter into profit maximization is that profit maximization shouldn't always be the only priority. I am suggesting that if the only focus is on financial profit maximization, the future profitability of the organization may not be sustainable. In other words, sometimes you need to spend money to make money, and ensuring your staff are fairly compensated and rewarded, that you are buying quality products and are delivering value to your clients, and that you are investing in the improvement and advancement of your business may be equally important to the long-term profitability and interest of the business.

Financial Model Review

As you will recall, in Chapter 5 we went into detail around what goes into your business's financial model. As a quick recap, there are three main components:

1. Revenue – The sales related to the product or service delivered

2. Direct costs – The costs directly associated with the delivery of the product or service. Examples of direct costs would include purchases (materials and supplies purchased to make a product that is sold) and direct labour (these would be the wages and benefits required to make a product or to deliver a service)

3. Fixed costs – These are costs that remain stable whether a business sells a million units or five units, and do not fluctuate when the volume of revenue changes. Examples of fixed costs would be rent, management wages, insurance, bank charges, etc.

Once again, you need to be familiar with your businesses financial model if you want to ensure that your profitability is being maximized. Now that you understand how the numbers work together, we will review where you need to look to find more profit in your current business operations.

Revenue

As you will recall in the prior chapter, there are only three ways to grow your revenue: number of customers, price, and frequency of purchases. Each of these three areas need to be reviewed to ensure that the lost opportunity of revenue is eliminated. Here are a few areas you should investigate:

- Customer retention – are you losing clients?
- Are you generating enough leads?
- Are you following up on these leads quickly and effectively?
- Is your sales closing process effective?
- Is your pricing correct? Are you missing out on the opportunity to charge more for your product or service?
- Are you not taking advantage of happy customers and missing out on upsell/resell/packaged pricing opportunities?

Variable Costs

If you can eliminate unnecessary costs associated with your product or service delivery, there is a significant upside to generating more profit for your business. This is true since every dollar saved on product savings or direct costs associated with delivering a specific product or service will be multiplied across every unit delivered. Ultimately, you will increase your profit margins, increase your business gross profit, and increase your bottom-line profitability. Here are a few areas to investigate with respect to variable costs:

- Excessive purchases costs – Are you paying too much for your product? Are there more cost-effective options?

- Increasing product and material costs – Are your product and material costs increasing? Are there any new potential sources of the product? Should you be considering a price increase to offset the cost? If your cost increases without increasing your revenue, the margins on your sales will be reduced.

- Staffing efficiency – Are your employee workflow processes efficient and optimal for the delivery of your product or service? Could they be improved so that you could increase the capacity for each employee to deliver more product or services?

- Outsourcing – Have you considered the option of outsourcing your production, direct wages, shipping costs, etc.? It may be possible that you can pay an outside organization to build or deliver a product or service at a more efficient cost than you can do internally.

- Benchmark wages – When you hire new employees or review existing employees' performance, you need to compare wages to industry standards. You may need to modify any future offers (or pay increases) should you determine that your wage costs are excessive.

- Review inventory shrinkage – Have you reviewed any inventory waste to determine if there is a more effective way to eliminate waste? Processes should be consistently reviewed to ensure the least amount of waste is realized.

- Mitigate loss and theft – Are sufficient safeguards in place to ensure that employees are not stealing product from your business?

Fixed Expenses

The cost of everything we buy consistently increases year after year. As is the case with your own business, suppliers will continue to increase prices until they have resistance. With that in mind, if you are interested in reducing your regular monthly operating expenses, it is necessary to test the market to see if there are more cost-effective options available. The ability to reduce your monthly expenses is important when considering profit maximization, as any monthly reductions you are able to generate will save you money every month going forward. Here are some areas to reduce your fixed costs:

- Renegotiate your lease – Depending on how the market is performing, it may be beneficial to renegotiate your lease for office space. If the market is suggesting that there are many vacant properties, it may be in the landlord's best interest to consider reducing your rent to keep you in their location.

- Shop your insurance to multiple providers – As your business grows, you have new assets, and your revenue increases, so too will your cost of insurance. With that said, there are numerous insurance providers who will be able to offer you similar policies. Insurance is one of those items that you want to consistently shop around to ensure you don't overpay for appropriate coverage or pay too much due to an excessive or unnecessary policy.

- Credit card processing – Many businesses take advantage of the cash management process of accepting credit cards for payments. Each year the processing fees seem to get hiked up. However, there are many different providers, and you should constantly shop rates and ensure your provider is aware of the other options you have available. The rates they issue you can always be negotiated.

Big versus Small – Keep It Simple

One thing that we need to get very clear is that the size of your revenue doesn't mean you make more money. Some of the most financially successful people I know don't have a big business. In fact, some of them don't even have an office or employees. I have provided an example below of the comparison between a complex business versus a simple business. At the end of the day, both businesses generate the same bottom-line income; however, the complex business has a significant number of more complicated factors in the business such as staffing, product costs, risk of lost product, shipping errors, etc. If one of the businesses was to be considered better, it would be the business that is simpler with less risk. Let's review the example now.

	Complex	Simple
REVENUE		
Product revenue	10,500,000.00	-
Service revenue	2,300,000.00	1,850,000.00
	12,800,000.00	1,850,000.00
VARIABLE COSTS		
Purchase of raw materials	2,100,000.00	-
Direct labor for assembly	1,575,000.00	-
Packaging	1,050,000.00	-
Wages and benefits (directly related to the product sale/delivery)	2,625,000.00	450,000.00
Supplies directly related to the delivery of the product	57,500.00	-

Shipping	525,000.00	-
Other direct sales costs (such as commissions, lead acquisition costs, etc.)	262,500.00	-
Vehicle costs (travel to deliver or sell the product)	440,000.00	-
Variable overhead costs	125,000.00	-
Total costs (NEED TO TOTAL THE BELOW PRE-DETERMINED TOTAL)	8,760,000.00	450,000.00
Gross profit	4,040,000.00	1,400,000.00
FIXED COSTS		
Advertising	350,000.00	75,000.00
Bank charges and interest	175,000.00	5,000.00
Insurance	45,000.00	12,500.00
Interest	97,500.00	6,500.00
Management wages	1,002,500.00	150,000.00
Office and general	48,500.00	12,500.00
Professional development	30,000.00	20,000.00
Professional fees	75,000.00	10,000.00
Property tax	185,000.00	-
Repairs and maintenance	365,000.00	7,000.00
Rent	420,000.00	48,000.00
Telephone	65,000.00	30,000.00
Travel and entertainment	46,500.00	15,000.00
Utilities	75,000.00	-
Vehicle	60,000.00	8,500.00
Total fixed costs	3,040,000.00	400,000.00
Income from operations	1,000,000.00	1,000,000.00

I share this example for a few reasons. Primarily, I want you to understand that bigger isn't always better. In fact, most often it is easier to make money when utilizing a simpler financial model. In many instances, people want to grow their business just to say they are growing. If the business is expanding and taking on additional risks, the reward at the end of the day should also increase. In order to ensure your business is ready to grow and realize improved financial results, the business needs to be tightened up and ready to maximize profitability.

One thing I will say about businesses that are bigger and have greater leverage with respect to staffing is that there tends to be greater opportunity to tighten up costs and improve process efficiency, which will result in significant profit improvement potential.

Profit Is a Good Thing

Many business owners would suggest that making money is not the number one priority with a business venture. Some would argue that what they deliver helps people, and that helping people is really the key driver of their business and making as much money as possible is not a priority. I respectfully disagree with anyone who thinks that profiting should not be the number one priority. And here is why: if you don't make a profit, there is no business, and if there is no business, you can't deliver your product or service that makes a difference in someone's life. In fact, I would argue that you, as a business owner, have a duty to be as financially profitable as possible so that you don't deprive the world of your offering and so that you can help as many people as you can. Lack of commitment to maximum profitability is then just a selfish act. In addition, the more profitable the business is, the more that you can reinvest into the business, investing in more human capital, in better equipment, in more product to deliver, and the list goes on. And as you reinvest in your business, you can help more people and have a greater impact in the world. So, the more money you make, the greater your impact will be in the lives of those you serve. If you are serious about delivering the most value and having the greatest impact, you will make profitability the number one priority. Again, *if your business doesn't profit, there is no business, and if there is no business, you can't make a difference in the lives of those you serve.*

CHAPTER 12:

Understanding Cash Flow

*"Never take your eyes off the cash flow
because it's the lifeblood of business."*
– Sir Richard Branson

In the last chapter, we reviewed the concept of profits and what an entrepreneur can do to ensure that business profits are being maximized. Once again, if a business isn't making a profit, there is no business, and there is no sustainability for the future life of the organization. The only area of the business that is more important than creating a profit is ensuring your business has a positive cash flow.

As a business advisor to entrepreneurs, one of the most common questions that arises is "My business made a great profit this year, my revenue grew, and my profit grew, but is that right? It doesn't seem to make sense because I should have money in the bank, and I don't. Shouldn't my profit be sitting in my bank account?"

One of the biggest misconceptions when understanding the financial results of a business is that if a business is profiting, everything will be okay. Let me be very clear here:

PROFIT ≠ CASH

There have been many incredible businesses in history who have been extremely profitable but have not survived because they ran out of cash. I'm sure you have heard people say, "Cash is king," and they are right. Without enough cash available inside the business, there is no business, even if the profit is there.

How Cash Is Impacted

To understand what you need to do to optimize the cash flow of your business, the first thing you need to understand is how cash is influenced.

Accounts Receivable

Accounts receivable are amounts that are owed to you based on making a sale that didn't involve the collection of money at the time of the transaction. Accounts receivable is the financing of your customer's purchase on their behalf, where they take possession of the product or service now and have a future obligation to pay.

Often if cash flow becomes a concern in a business, it is due to poor cash collection practices. In other words, you continue to sell your product, but you aren't good at collecting the money for it. If you don't collect the money related to the sale, the future success of the business is in real jeopardy.

Accounts receivable has a two-sided effect on the cash flow of a business. When a sale is made and cash is not collected, it has a negative impact on cash flow. For example, if the company sells a product for $100, the profit is $100. Certainly, it is profitable, but to convert that into cash flow, we need to reduce the profit by the fact that our accounts receivable increased by $100, resulting in our cash flow being zero. Conversely, we could sell nothing for the month, our profits are zero, but we collected $100 from a customer sale from the previous month. In this case, profit is zero, but cash flow is a positive $100.

As you can probably tell, cash collection of your accounts receivable could be a very positive way to improve the cash balances in your business. A few ways to improve the collection of accounts receivable would be to introduce the acceptance of additional sources of payment such as credit cards, online payments, and preauthorized payments. The quicker you can convert accounts receivable to cash, the quicker you can take your business to being flush with cash.

Prepaid Items

At certain points in the business cycle, it is required for you to pay for a future expense in advance, meaning that you are prepaying for future use. A few examples of prepaid items would be:

- Rent – Requiring your first and last month's rent up front, prior to occupying a space, is a common practice for most landlords.

- Insurance – If you choose to pay for your entire insurance policy at the start of the year (instead of paying for it monthly) you are prepaying for the year's insurance costs prior to them being incurred. The result is that the insurance expense would be calculated each month, but up front, the entire amount would be prepaid and not hit your expenses until it is used.

- Travel costs – In many instances, we pay in advance for any flights or travel packages, only to use them at a future date. In this case, the travel costs would sit as a prepaid item, and would be expensed during the period of actual travel.

- Membership fees – Many membership costs are on an annual basis and are paid up front. Since the benefits of membership will take place over the next twelve-month period, the up-front cost would be considered a prepaid item.

The importance of understanding prepaid items is that they will not show up as an expense on your income statement, meaning that you don't see a deduction in the business at the time of payment; however, they are paid for, meaning that the profits won't reflect these costs, but the cash will be impacted in a negative way. For example, let's say the business made a $100 sale during the month and collected the cash for it, leaving the business with $100 in profits and cash flow of $100. During the same period, you paid $100 for travel costs that will happen six months from now. The result is that the profit is still $100, but your cash is back to zero.

It is important to understand the relationship with prepaids and cash so that you can be mindful of the cash implications of such items

Inventory

Inventory is the accumulation of items on hand that you have available for sale to your customers. A good example of inventory would be cars on a dealership lot (unless you are following the Tesla model of online sales only and no inventory on hand). In many businesses, it is imperative that you have available items for your customers to purchase. In fact, if you don't have items available, your customers will go elsewhere to find what they are looking for. For those businesses who have and manage inventory, as they grow their business, so too does their inventory. This happens so that they continue to have products available for their growing customer base to purchase.

However, increasing inventory has a negative relationship with cash. For example, the business makes a $100 sale, and collects the money up front. The profit of the business is $100; however, in growing their business, they have decided to buy more items to have available to their customers. In doing so, they spend $100 on purchasing additional new items to sell. The result, the profit is still $100, but the cash is zero.

If you are in a business that maintains inventory, it is very important that you manage your inventory increases carefully to ensure that you don't have an abundance of items to sell, but no way to pay for them or other expenses. We will discuss ways to plan for this later in the chapter.

Capital Purchases

In many businesses it is necessary to invest in assets that are required to deliver your sales. For example, many businesses require vehicles to travel, computers and technology to process information, buildings to operate out of, desks and chairs for the office, and specialized high value equipment that is used to deliver a service to your customers. Many times, especially for smaller items, businesses will purchase these items with cash that is in the account. However, this is not a deduction in the business, as it has a future value and is considered an asset in the business. So, if we go back to our sales example of the $100, the company sells $100 of product during the month and collects the money. Profit is currently $100, and cash is $100. If we then go out and buy a new computer for $100, the business still has a profit of $100, but the cash is zero.

Many, growing businesses require a continuous reinvestment in capital purchases and improvements for the future. However, you need to be conscious of the cash impacts of these types of investments, and know that your business may be profiting, but if you continue to reinvest all the profits into new assets, there may be no cash left to operate the business.

Accounts Payable

Accounts payable are comprised of items that you have received a benefit for but have not yet paid for. Accounts payable have the reverse relationship to cash as compared to accounts receivable, meaning that the higher your accounts payable, the better your cash management has been with your ability to get the benefit for a product or service but to keep the cash related to the payment of that product or service in the bank account until a future date. Items that would be considered accounts payable could include trade payables, income taxes, employee deductions, etc.

In our $100 example, consider that your business makes a sale for $100, and in order to make that sale, you had to buy inventory for $50. The profit in this situation is $50. However, you didn't pay the $50, instead you made an arrangement that you would receive the inventory now, but would pay for it at a later date. In this case, you have a profit of $50, but you have cash in the bank of $100. Thus, the more you can avoid payment up front and defer it for a later date, the better immediate cash position you will have.

However, there is a negative concern related to accounts payable. For example, let's review the same sale for $100 with $50 profit. Again, we have arranged to pay the $50 at a later date, however, we also needed to pay $100 related to an amount we owed from the prior month. In this situation, we have profit of $50, but zero cash. In this case, because we had an amount payable, it may have been a benefit up front, but when we had to pay it, it drained our cash flow then.

Sometimes business owners take advantage of deferring payment, utilizing accounts payable to their vendors, but have spent cash on new equipment or inventory (like we previously discussed) and the cash the business saved by not paying their vendors has now been used in other areas. Thus, there is no cash to pay the vendors when the bill comes due. Cash management related to accounts payable is very important. Even though you may be able to retain your cash by utilizing these arrangements, it is important that you be mindful of the future obligations and make sure you have the cash resources available to make the required future payments.

Gift Certificates/Unearned Revenue

Receiving up-front payments for any service or product to be delivered later is one of the best cash management tools you have available. Selling gift cards or receiving a deposit for future work allows a business to receive cash up front, with the obligation of delivering something at a later time. Let's look at our example again. Your business makes a sale for $100 and collects the cash. The total profit is $100, and your cash is $100. In addition, you received a deposit up front for a sale to happen next month. In this case, your profit is still $100, but now your cash is $200.

Similar to the risk of accounts payable, if you receive the cash up front, you need to ensure you have the cash available to deliver on your product or service when required. In some instances, I have seen that businesses take the $100 up front, but spend it on a new piece of equipment, leaving the business with zero cash. The problem is that to deliver on the $100 sale, it may cost $50 to buy the product, but the business doesn't have the necessary cash resources to pay for it. Although advanced deposits are a very beneficial cash management process (much better than having accounts receivable), it

110

is important to be mindful of the future delivery obligations and to manage cash resources for those future needs.

Owner Advances

One area where cash seems to disappear is in the owner's pocket. I often hear from business owners that the company is profitable, but there is no money left in the bank, so the profits must be wrong. Only to discover that when profits were created, it was being syphoned into the owner's personal bank account. On the one hand, it is their business, right? So why shouldn't they have it? And I don't completely disagree. If you want to generate business profits to have access to funds that will improve your personal lifestyle, that is fine by me. However, if you are drawing the profits out of the business and not paying the appropriate tax deductions on that income, it could put you and your business in a cash constraint. For example, the business makes a sale of $100, and the profit is $100 for the month. At the same time, the owner draws out the $100, leaving the company with zero cash. At the end of the month however, the company needs to pay tax on the $100 profit and has no money to do so and is now in a negative cash position. Another even more dangerous example is if the company had $100 sale, with $100 profit, and received a $100 deposit up front for a future job, leaving the company with $100 profit, and $200 in cash. Well, the business owner takes out $200 and spends it personally. When the company is due to pay tax on the $100 profits, there is nothing left. In addition, when the company goes to deliver the product for the $100 deposit, the customer decides they no longer want it and request a refund. Now the business is in a major situation, still owing tax money, and not having sufficient cash to refund the customer.

111

The main objective of understanding owner advances is to suggest that even when there is cash in the account, you need to make sure that your future obligations are arranged prior to draining the business of all its cash resources.

Debt

Borrowing money is one of the quickest ways to improve the cash position of a business. Although many entrepreneurs have a fear of borrowing money, it can be a very useful resource for a growing business. In fact, many of the items we discussed previously, such as accounts receivable, inventory, and capital additions, can all be financed with the use of a debt instrument. What this does is allow for an increase in inventory and purchase of capital items, without worrying about draining the immediate cash resources of the business. Again, the use of debt instruments can be a very proactive means to reinvesting in your business without draining the cash resources of the company.

One item that you need to consider is that at some point, all debt needs to be repaid. This means that cash may come in now to help finance the current cash needs of the business; however, in the near future, cash resources are going to need to be drawn out to repay this obligation.

Here is our debt example. In the current month, we make a sale for $100 and collect the cash. Thus, profit is $100, and cash is $100. We then want to purchase additional inventory for $100, which would leave us with zero cash. However, we decide to borrow $100 to finance the inventory increase, which leaves us with $100 of cash and $100 of profit. In the next month, we have no sales, but we need to start repaying our debt obligation. We need to repay $20 per month over five months to pay the debt off. So, our cash is drained down to $80, and will continue to be drained by $20 per month. If we have any other obligations such as paying down our accounts payable, or taxes etc., we could find ourselves in a tight cash situation, because we need to find a way to create an additional $20 per month in cash to pay the debt off.

Again, debt can be a very useful tool to allow for the growth of a business while effectively managing the cash resources of a business. At the same time, it is essential that you are mindful about the future payments to repay the debt and how that will have an impact on the cash flow of the business.

Profit

Although we can agree that profit ≠ cash, one thing is for sure, by making sales, and generating a profit, it provides the business with a great start to generating positive cash flow inside the business. The important part to remember is that if accounts receivable don't exist, no inventory or capital obligations are happening, and there are no cash resources required to repay liabilities, then the cash flow of the business will be strong. Profit is a great start to establishing positive cash flow inside the business, but on its own, is not enough.

Below is a summary of how a business's cash flow can be impacted by the above items.

Company Cash Flow Analysis Monthly

Net income (from actual results)	$ XXX,XXX
Additions to cash:	
Amortization/depreciation	$ XXX,XXX
Decrease in accounts receivable	$ XXX,XXX
Decrease in inventory	$ XXX,XXX
Increase in accounts payable	$ XXX,XXX
Increase in taxes payable	$ XXX,XXX
Financing received	$ XXX,XXX
	$ XXX,XXX
Subtractions from cash	
Increase in accounts receivable	$ XXX,XXX
Increase in inventory	$ XXX,XXX
Decrease in accounts payable	$ XXX,XXX
Decrease taxes payable	$ XXX,XXX
Asset purchases	$ XXX,XXX
Debt repayment	$ XXX,XXX
Shareholder payments	$ XXX,XXX
	$ XXX,XXX

Maximize Cash Flow with Effective Cash Management

Now that you understand some of the major impacts on the cash flow of your business, what are some policies or processes that you could put in place to ensure the cash flow of your business is optimized? If you get your cash management policies in place to ensure effective cash collection, you will be positioned well to ensure that the cash flow of your business is strong.

1. Cash collection policy – As we previously discussed, the mitigation of or entire elimination of accounts receivable would be a very positive step toward optimizing the cash management of your business. Here are some ideas on how to reduce or eliminate accounts receivable in your business:

   a. Accept multiple forms of payment – You need to make it as easy as possible for customers to pay you. Here are some ideas to implement:
      - Credit cards
      - Cash
      - Cheques
      - Electronic funds transfers
      - Wire payments
      - Online banking payments

   b. Collect money at the time of the sale – Put in place a company policy that you will not deliver a product or service without payment at the time of delivery. One way to ensure this happens is to collect credit card information prior to delivery to ensure that once the product or service has been delivered, you can process payment.

   c. Collect money prior to the sale (gift cards, deposits in advance) – As we discussed earlier, the acceptance of cash in advance is a proactive cash management process that will ensure maximum cash flow in your business. If there is an opportunity to get full or partial payment prior to delivering your product or service, this will put your business in a great cash flow position.

2. Financing – Although many entrepreneurs don't look favourably at financing solutions due to the idea of running their business without debt, the use of financing can be a very positive solution to growing your business without draining all the cash resources of the company. Here are a few ideas for introducing financing:

    a. Working capital cash management (line of credit) – This type of financing solution can typically be arranged related to financing your accounts receivable (where the bank provides cash in advance to allow you to sell to your clients on a receivable basis), or to finance the increase in inventory. Again, both accounts receivable and inventory increases can drain the cash resources of a business, and if you continue to grow, the use of a line of credit may provide you with the cash resources you need to continue to invest in this growth.

    b. Borrowing for capital purchases – Long-term debt financing for equipment and other capital items allows the business to invest in this new revenue-driving resource and allows you to use the new profits to pay for it in the future. If you continue to invest in new equipment, this type of debt financing will allow for the equipment to pay for itself, while you add additional profit and cash flow to the business operations.

3. Payable management – As we discussed earlier, deferring paying for items that you receive a benefit on now, with payment arranged at a future date, is a very proactive method of cash management. In fact, if you can use the resources you have received the benefit of to generate income and positive

cash in the business, you can then allow these resources to pay for themselves by delaying payment. Once again, delaying payment is a positive cash management process – just be cautious not to get in a position in which payment of obligations in the future causes a cash flow concern at that time.

4. Cash flow smoothing – One area of cash management that I strongly advocate for is the smoothing of cash flow. What I mean here is that it is beneficial to arrange it so that smaller consistent cash outflows are arranged so that you avoid any major outflow surprises that can put your business in a bad position. Some examples of how to approach this are as follows:
   a. Turn annual costs into monthly payments (avoid paying up front)
   b. Pay sales tax obligations monthly (instead of quarterly or annually)
   c. Pay income tax instalments regularly (instead of a big balance at the end of the year)
   d. Set up debt financing repayments to be weekly instead of monthly

The key to operating a successful business is to ensure that you have an effective cash management process in place to maintain a healthy cash flow for the business. If the company is making a profit, and effective cash management is in place, your business will be set up for future financial success and will realize extraordinary financial results.

CHAPTER 13:

Minimize Your Taxes

"The hardest thing to understand
in the world is income tax."
– Albert Einstein

In my Vision to Results framework guiding entrepreneurs to realizing extraordinary results, much of the discussion has been around how to outline your business goals and how to maximize the business performance, which includes profit maximization and cash flow management. One of the key aspects of driving maximum business performance is making sure that there is a plan in place to ensure that you keep as much of it as possible. This means once you make it, how do you keep it so that the tax man doesn't get more than they should?

As a partner with Tony Robbins and his Global Accounting Advisors, we conducted research around the risk of loss due to excessive tax costs in a business, and the results were staggering. We met with thousands of entrepreneurs from across the globe, reviewed their tax findings, and discovered this:

92% of businesses were paying more tax than was legally required.

I was blown away with this discovery and realized quickly that there is a major issue with tax loss for entrepreneurs, which will quickly take away from your ability to maximize the impact of your business and will certainly take away from the extraordinary financial results you are creating.

How much does it cost you if you pay too much tax? I have calculated an example below, demonstrating the cost of paying $5,000 a year over a period of ten years. The total cost to your business would be over $155,000. That is a significant amount of money! The assumptions of this calculation would be that this money wasn't available to reinvest in your business, which typically returns a profit of a 20% return (based on the risk and reward of entrepreneurship). The compound effect of this loss is a significant number. And if I'm being honest, our team almost always finds a minimum of $5,000 in tax savings with any client we work with.

In working with Tony, and to eliminate the risk of tax loss, we created a free tax review program that allows entrepreneurs to have certainty around whether they are part of the 92% or one of the 8% who are not overpaying. We have been committed to eliminating excessive tax on entrepreneurs, and continue to offer this service. I invite you to book a free tax review appointment here: gauvreaucpa.ca/the-wealthy-entrepreneur/resources.

Since there is such a risk of tax loss for entrepreneurs, we will now review some areas that, if planned proactively, can save you a significant amount of money, will allow for an increased impact, and will be a massive contributor to realizing extraordinary financial results.

The cost of too much tax

	Year 1	Year 2	Year 3	Year 4	Year 5	Year 6	Year 7	Year 8	Year 9	Year 10	Total
Year 1	5,000	6,000	7,200	8,640	10,368	12.442	14,930	17,916	21,499	25,799	30,959
Year 2		5,000	6,000	7,200	8,640	10,368	12,442	14,930	17,916	21,499	25,799
Year 3			5,000	6,000	7,200	8,640	10,368	12,442	14,930	17,916	21,499
Year 4				5,000	6,000	7,200	8,640	10,368	12,442	14,930	17,916
Year 5					5,000	6,000	7,200	8,640	10,368	12,442	14,930
Year 6						5,000	6,000	7,200	8,640	10,368	12,442
Year 7							5,000	6,000	7,200	8,640	10,368
Year 8								5,000	6,000	7,200	8,640
Year 9									5,000	6,000	7,200
Year 10										5,000	6,000
Total	5,000	11,000	18,200	26,840	37,208	49,650	64,580	82,495	103,995	129,793	155,752

Business Structures

How a company is organized may be the most important proactive tax planning concept available to entrepreneurs. Later in the chapter, we will discuss an overview of the personal and corporate tax rates, which are provided as a guide to manage expectations of future liabilities, but also know that how you structure your income may have a major impact on your tax required on your business income. We will now look further into the structures available for you to operate your business.

1. **Sole Proprietorship**

   Sole proprietorship is the simplest structure to operate your business from. There is no formal procedure to form a sole proprietorship and there are few formal accounting requirements. There is no separate tax filing required as the income earned from a sole proprietorship is included on your personal income tax return. You can easily exchange personal and business assets.

   There are a few downsides to a sole proprietorship. Personal liability and lack of formal protection is a major concern as all the business's assets and the operation of the business are susceptible to risk and exposure, and so too are all the personal assets of the business owner. The second concern is that since the income is reported with your other personal income, the business is susceptible to personal tax rates, which are always higher than the tax you would pay inside a corporate entity.

   This is a major opportunity for tax planning, to ensure that the entity is utilizing the most favourable tax treatment for future tax obligations

2. **Partnership**

The use of a partnership is very similar to a sole proprietorship, with the one difference being that there are multiple parties involved in the business ownership. As was the case with the sole proprietorship, personal liability and lack of formal protection is a major concern. There is an option to form a limited liability partnership (LLP), which may allow for each partner to not be liable for the obligations and liabilities arising from the actions of the other partners. If you were looking to form a partnership, and an LLP is an option, this would be something you should consider to mitigate the personal liability exposure of operating a business in a partnership.

In addition, as was the case with the sole proprietorship, the income earned from the partnership is reported with your other personal income, which means that the business is once again susceptible to personal tax rates, which are always higher than the tax you would pay inside a corporate entity.

This is a situation where there is an opportunity for tax planning and to ensure that the entity is utilizing the most favourable tax treatment for future tax obligations

3. **Limited Liability Company (US only)**

The Limited Liability Company (LLC) is probably the best-known corporate entity other than a regular corporation. It's a hybrid entity that offers the liability protection of a C corporation with the tax option to be treated as a partnership or a corporation.

An LLC can be structured for additional flexibility and may include unlimited members. An LLC also provides ease of operation and possibilities for expansion, which makes it attractive for smaller business operations.

When operating in an LLC, liability is limited in much the same way as with a C corporation. This means that so long as you file your taxes appropriately, your liability will largely be limited to your business assets and will protect your personal assets.

4. Corporation (also known as a C corporation in the US)

A corporation is a separate legal entity that has the responsibility for filing its own business tax returns and paying the respective business taxes related to this income. The advantages of a corporation include liability protection for its shareholders, the flexibility to easily transfer ownership of the corporate shares, and favourable tax treatment for certain expenses.

There are additional filing costs and complexities; however, if the business is earning income or is planning to generate extraordinary financial results, a corporate structure should be strongly considered to ensure that the business is structured in the most efficient way for tax mitigation.

5. S Corporation

The S corporation is another special form of corporation that operates like a C corporation but is taxed like a partnership. There are strict limitations on the structure of an S corporation, including the number and types of shareholders.

The S corporation is considered a good vehicle for small, closely held corporations. One of the most attractive features of the S corporation is the ability to "slice up" distributions to shareholders and reclassify those distributions.

Compensation Strategies

One of the ways that you can proactively plan for tax minimization is to ensure that your personal compensation strategy is well thought out, because different types of income generate different tax implications. Here are a few of the most common ways to compensate the owners of the business.

1. **Unincorporated Businesses**

   As was discussed above, if you are not set up as a corporation or an LLC, all your business income will be taxed with on your personal income tax return. The benefit of earning income this way is that it is simplified and eliminates the need to file a separate tax return. However, by earning income this way, it also makes you responsible to pay income tax based on personal tax rates. If you are earning income in your business, you should consider whether it is better for you to include it personally, or to consider another structure.

2. **Salary**

   To earn a salary is to be paid as an employee of a corporation. In this situation, the corporation gets a deduction for the earnings that you are paid, which reduces the businesses taxable income; however, it is added to your personal income, and taxed accordingly. There are benefits related to the use of a salary for business tax planning purposes (such as issuing a year-end bonus to reduce the current tax obligation and pushing the tax obligation into a future tax year).

3. **Dividends**

   To earn a dividend is to be compensated as a shareholder or an investor in the corporation. In this instance, the business does not get a taxable deduction related to this type of compensation; however, the shareholder, when claiming this income on their personal taxes, would have a reduced personal tax rate, to avoid the potential of double taxation. In many instances, by utilizing a dividend (as opposed to a salary) the corporation may be able to save on employee benefits and required government contributions for employment income. The use of dividends should be reviewed to see if there are opportunities to save tax in the overall business and personal situations.

How Tax Rates Work

Now that we have talked about the different business structures that are available, you need to be aware of the different rates that apply to each type of business structure, as well as different compensation strategies.

Although I don't want to get too in depth related to the overall tax rates of businesses and individuals, it is important to understand the difference between taxes paid on corporate tax versus the taxes paid as a sole proprietor or partner in a business.

Personal tax rates – Personal tax rates apply to every individual who earns taxable income from sources of employment, investment income, or self-employed income. The personal tax rates are different across countries and in the state or province where you reside. What you need to know is what the top personal tax rates are on your income, so that you can properly plan for future tax obligations. Below is a summary of the tax rates across Canada and the United States of America:

- Personal tax – Canada

  o Federal – the top federal tax rate in Canada is 33% on income over $200,000
  o Provincial/territorial – the top provincial or territorial tax rates in Canada range from 11.5% in Nunavut to 25.75% in Quebec
  o Total – this would put the top income earners in a top tax bracket in Canada of 44.5% to 58.75%

- Personal tax – United States of America

  o Federal – the top federal tax rate in the US is 37% and is effective at different income levels, depending on filing single or jointly
  o State – there is a major range in state personal tax rates in the US. Some states apply no income tax, some apply a flat tax rate, and others apply a marginal rate, topped by the state of California at a rate of 13.3%
  o Total – this would put the top income earners in a top tax bracket across the US of 37% to 50.3%

- Corporate tax – Canada

  o Federal – for Canadian Controlled Private Corporations, the federal tax rate is 9% on income up to $500,000 and increases to 15% for income over $500,000
  o Provincial/territorial – the corporate tax rates are different across provinces and territories; however, the respective rates range from 0% to 4% across the country for the first

$500,000 in income, and increase to a range of 8.5% to 22% based on the location of the business

o Total – corporate tax rates range, depending on the location, from 9% to 11% for the first $500,000, and increase to a rate of 26% to 31% for income above $500,000

- Corporate tax – United States of America

  o Federal – the US tax on corporate income was reduced to 21% federally in 2017
  o State – forty-four states levy a corporate income tax, ranging from 2.5% to 12% depending on the location of the business and its corporate filing
  o Total – corporate tax rates range, depending on the location, from 23.5% to 33%

I summarize the above rates so that you are fully aware of the expectations of your business and personal tax, and to ensure you are appropriately planning to mitigate any tax liabilities to maximize your future savings. This will just give you an idea of what you are up against, and how the overall tax system works in North America.

What Can I Deduct as an Expense in My Business?

A general rule of thumb related to what is deductible would be that if an expense is incurred related to the development of business or the delivery of its product or services to its customers, then it is deductible. There are some exceptions such as golf dues (not deductible) as well as meals and entertainment (which are only 50% deductible); however, most items are fully deductible. Here is a list of some items to consider to ensure that you are getting the full deductibility of business expenses and are well on your way to mitigating your tax liabilities:

- Advertising
- Bad debts
- Bank charges
- Delivery costs
- Depreciation of capital assets (equipment, furniture, vehicles, etc.)
- Dues and memberships
- Insurance
- Interest
- Meals and entertainment (50%)
- Office expenses
- Office supplies
- Professional development
- Professional fees
- Management and administration costs
- Purchases of materials and supplies
- Rent
- Repairs and maintenance
- Property taxes
- Subcontractors
- Travel expenses
- Utilities
- Vehicle expenses
- Wages and benefits

The goal of this chapter is to introduce you to the idea of taxes on business income, and how the overall tax system is very complex and needs to be properly planned for to ensure you are maximizing your available deductions, mitigating your taxable income, and ensuring the appropriate business structure and compensation model is being utilized.

It is imperative that you find a professional you trust and who is willing to work proactively with you to ensure that the next step of your business is planned for and that you don't have any losses of wealth accumulation due to excessive tax costs. In essence, you want to make sure that you are not one of the 92% of business owners who are paying more tax than you legally have to. It all starts with a good plan followed by the necessary execution. If you are worried that you may be part of the 92%, my team at www.GauvreauCPA.ca would be happy to help.

CHAPTER 14:

Building Wealth

"The philosophy of the rich and the poor is this: the rich invest their money and spend what is left. The poor spend their money and invest what is left."
– Robert Kiyosaki

Up to this point, we have outlined what your business needs to do to realize extraordinary financial results, including the outline of your goals, creating the map of how to get there, designing the critical drivers, and staying accountable to realizing results. In addition, we have discussed how to maximize the profits in your business, how to maximize the cash flow in your business, and most recently, how you proactively plan to mitigate your tax liability to ensure you keep as much of your hard-earned money as possible. The last piece of the puzzle is understanding what you need to do to turn your business earnings into wealth creation and how you establish a path to realizing incredible wealth and financial freedom in your life.

Personal Budgeting

The most effective way to ensure you are accumulating personal wealth and savings is to outline the pathway to how you get there. This can be accomplished by preparing a personal budget. By establishing how much money is coming in and how much money is going out, you can determine how much excess cash you have available to support the financial requirements for your retirement, and how much excess cash you have available to indulge in extra items. When creating a budget, we also become very clear on how much we are spending and can make conscious decisions to cut back in areas where excessive spending has occurred.

Once you have a personal budget prepared, you know how much you need to pull from the business to ensure that your lifestyle costs are taken care of. Here's the deal, I'm not suggesting that you can't live an extravagant lifestyle, I am just saying that once you fully understand the costs associated with living the life you choose, you can determine how much needs to come from the business to support that lifestyle, and from there, you can determine how much is left in the business. Once you can determine what the cash requirements are for your business, you can establish how much excess cash is available to start the savings plan and begin the accumulation of serious wealth.

Psychology of Spending

The psychology of spending suggests that if someone has money in their account, and they have access to it, that they will most likely spend it instead of letting it accumulate. Once you have a personal budget and you understand the cash flow needs of the business, you can establish how much you can earmark to pull out of the business account. The psychology of moving it from your business chequing account into an investment account, and your inability to observe it and/or have ongoing access to it, will allow you to remove it from your mindset, which means you will not incur additional spending due to lack of available resources. This doesn't mean that if the business needed it, it couldn't be accessed; however, you don't want to make it so that you can easily observe it and access it.

The Power of Forced Savings

One of the easiest strategies to implement in your business is the idea of forced savings. We previously discussed cash flow and the concept of regular and frequent outgoing payments so as to smooth the outgoing cash flow and normalize the cash expectations in the business, now we want to take this a step further. What you want to do is set up a frequent, regular transfer from your business chequing account into your investment account. You can start with a low amount, say $100 per week, which would be set to occur the same day as a regular business deposit, so that you don't even really notice the $100 leaving the business. If you were to establish this in your business starting today, at this point next year you would have $5,200 in your investment account. The goal in this situation is to start with $100, and if the cash flow of the business is unaffected, then increase it to $200 per week. Continue with this process until it starts to become noticeable that the bank balance is getting slightly drained, and then back it off a little bit. Just imagine if you were able to increase it from $100 a week to $1,000 per week. Instead of $5,200 being saved, you are now looking at $52,000 saved. This is a massive step toward creating incredible wealth and a future of financial freedom.

One point of clarification in setting this process up is that we want to ensure the investments are being held within the business (not personally). Depending on your business structure, there may be significant tax advantages to holding these investments inside the business instead of personally. In the situation where it is a corporate structure, there are two types of tax that occur. First is tax on the business income, and second is tax to the business owner for pulling the money out of the business. If you establish the investments inside the company, you avoid the immediate taxation of the second portion, and you are starting with a higher initial investment, which will grow at a faster rate.

Investment Compounding

Now that you have set up a forced savings plan, at whatever regular transfer amount makes the most sense for the business, you can establish a plan on what to do with it. At this point, you are in a great position to have your money make money for you. If you just leave the money in your account, it will only increase by the amount you contribute. If you decide to invest it, you have the ability for your money to grow at an exponential rate.

If you were to be able to get your company to a point where you were able to save $52,000 per year (or $1,000 per week) you can see below the impact and exponential growth available to having these funds invested. The first example looks at the $52,000 per year, with an investment return of 5%. At the end of ten years, you would accumulate investments of $686,753. As a comparable calculation, I included an example of $52,000 per year, with an investment return of 10%. At the end of the ten years, and with earning a 10% return, you would accumulate investments of $911,621. As you can see, when

Compounding income

5% return on investment

	Year 1	Year 2	Year 3	Year 4	Year 5	Year 6	Year 7	Year 8	Year 9	Year 10	Total
Year 1	52,000	54,600	57,330	60,197	63,206	66,367	69,685	73,169	76,828	80,669	84,703
Year 2		52,000	54,600	57,330	60,197	63,206	66,367	69,685	73,169	76,828	80,669
Year 3			52,000	54,600	57,330	60,197	63,206	66,367	69,685	73,169	76,828
Year 4				52,000	54,600	57,330	60,197	63,206	66,367	69,685	73,169
Year 5					52,000	54,600	57,330	60,197	63,206	66,367	69,685
Year 6						52,000	54,600	57,330	60,197	63,206	66,367
Year 7							52,000	54,600	57,330	60,197	63,206
Year 8								52,000	54,600	57,330	60,197
Year 9									52,000	54,600	57,330
Year 10										52,000	54,600
Total	52,000	106,600	163,930	224,127	287,333	353,700	423,385	496,554	573,382	654,051	686,754

Compounding income

10% return on investment

	Year 1	Year 2	Year 3	Year 4	Year 5	Year 6	Year 7	Year 8	Year 9	Year 10	Total
Year 1	52,000	57,200	62,920	69,212	76,133	83,747	92,121	101,333	111,467	122,613	134,875
Year 2		52,000	57,200	62,920	69,212	76,133	83,747	92,121	101,333	111,467	122,613
Year 3			52,000	57,200	62,920	69,212	76,133	83,747	92,121	101,333	111,467
Year 4				52,000	57,200	62,920	69,212	76,133	83,747	92,121	101,333
Year 5					52,000	57,200	62,920	69,212	76,133	83,747	92,121
Year 6						52,000	57,200	62,920	69,212	76,133	83,747
Year 7							52,000	57,200	62,920	69,212	76,133
Year 8								52,000	57,200	62,920	69,212
Year 9									52,000	57,200	69,920
Year 10										52,000	57,200
Total	52,000	109,200	172,120	241,332	317,465	401,212	493,333	594,666	706,133	828,746	918,621

the investment is earning more, and reinvesting along the way, the higher the earnings and contributions up front, the faster will be the exponential growth of the wealth.

It should also be noted in these examples that I am assuming that these $52,000 contributions are being put into an investment on an annual basis. If we were to invest the $1,000 per week, you would take advantage of additional compounding, and the examples below would realize even larger exponential growth.

Investment Options

At this point we have established that having your money invested, even if it earns a conservative investment return, allows for a greater accumulation of wealth, and the compound effect of having these funds invested is a positive move toward creating greater wealth. In an effort to get you started with a few ideas on how to invest your surplus funds, we will now review a few commonly used investment options, which will allow you to get your money invested and starting to grow at an exponential rate.

- Mutual funds – A mutual fund is a type of investment vehicle consisting of a portfolio of stocks, bonds, or other securities. Mutual funds give small or individual investors access to diversified, professionally managed portfolios at a low price.

- Stocks – An equity investment generally refers to the buying and holding of shares of stock on a stock market by individuals and firms in anticipation of income from dividends and capital gains. Share investments are either bought and sold on stock exchanges or can be investments in shares of a private company. Historically, equity investments have outperformed most other investments over the long run.

- Index funds – An index fund is a portfolio of stocks or bonds designed to mimic the composition and performance of a financial market index. Index funds have lower expenses and fees than actively managed funds. The purpose of these investments is to follow the ups and downs of the particular stock market instead of a particular stock choice.

- Real estate – A real estate investment would involve the purchase of land and/or buildings that would either be residential, commercial, or institutional in nature. The goal would be to generate income by renting the facility to a tenant or group of tenants which would provide for a profit. In addition, there is a secondary benefit of owning real estate, in that there is an anticipation that the value of the land and building will also increase in value, offering an additional return for the investment.

- Insurance – There are some instances where insurance vehicles may make sense as an investment opportunity. In fact, there are insurance policies referred to as whole life or universal life policies that allow for investments to be held within an insurance policy. One of the benefits to this type of investment opportunity would be that it protects the investor and their family should any sudden loss of life occur, and because the investments are held within the insurance policy, there is no taxable income related to the earnings in these investments, leaving the earnings to continue to compound inside the insurance vehicle for the long-term. These aren't a good fit for everyone, but they are certainly an option.

Some considerations around your investment options:

1. Tax implications – Different investments have different tax implications. For example, dividends and capital gains are taxed more favourably than interest or rental income, whereas investments inside an insurance policy may avoid tax altogether. It is important to look at an investment for its long-term after-tax return.

2. Fees – Tony Robbins speaks to this in great detail in his most recent book *Unshakeable*. In short, different investment options, such as mutual funds, carry high costs associated with their ongoing management. These fees significantly reduce the overall return on investment, whereas an index fund, a similar type of investment, would have a substantially reduced fee associated with its ongoing management. It is important to understand the costs associated with each.

3. Time requirement – One aspect of an investment that you need to consider is how much time and attention it is going to take from you. If you are driving a business, you may not have a significant amount of time to manage a residential rental property with multiple tenants, and deal with plumbing, painting, and ongoing maintenance and headaches.

Whatever you decide to invest in, the goal is to make sure that you are investing in something that has a reasonable risk/reward profile. Depending on the stage of your life, the ability to invest in a riskier opportunity may or may not make sense. Typically, younger investors tend to take greater risk, investing in equity investments with a higher risk profile. This is because if the investment has an issue in the short-term, the young investor has the ability to let this investment recover over a longer period. On the other side, more mature investors may want to mitigate their risk exposure since their ability to play the long game with investments may not be a possibility. At the end of the day, you need to pick an investment that best suits you, and one that will provide you a reasonable return based on your risk tolerance. Keep in mind that if you are looking to make higher-risk investments, the reward potential on the other side should outweigh the risk. If it doesn't, find a lower risk investment that will provide the opportunity for those same rewards.

Value of Your Business

At the end of the day, you now understand that there are options to make your money grow at an exponential rate. However, keep in mind that the greatest potential earning vehicle will always be your business. If you follow the Vision to Results framework, you will realize extraordinary financial results in your business, and will generate a significant return on investment. At the same time, you don't want to lose focus on your business since it will always have your highest income earning potential. Priority number one should be ensuring your business is running seamlessly; however, if you can find an investment with a good return, with moderate risk, that will not require you to lose focus on running your business, you should consider how to get it implemented so that you can create exponential wealth and start on your path toward financial freedom.

CHAPTER 15:

Realizing Extraordinary Financial Results

"An investment in knowledge
pays the best interest."
– Benjamin Franklin

At this point you should be very clear about how to execute a plan to realize extraordinary financial results in your business. The reality is, if you fully implement the framework and concepts discussed in *The Wealthy Entrepreneur,* your business will make more money, have a bigger impact, and will provide for a future of wealth and financial freedom for you and your family.

There have been many books written on the topic of entrepreneurship; however, *The Wealthy Entrepreneur* focuses on my experience of working with over 500 entrepreneurs, learning from those experiences and from the professionals they engage to take them to the next level, and presents an implementable framework that outlines specific and measurable steps for creating extraordinary financial results. The question you need to ask yourself is this: do I want to implement this framework myself, or do I want to work with a team who will deliver these results for my business? Regardless of your approach, any progress that you make will be the result of fully implementing this framework in your business, and if you do, you will be on track to achieve extraordinary financial results.

The combination of outlining your vision, understanding your business's financial model, predicting your future results, outlining key metrics, creating a scoreboard, and staying accountable to your vision by measuring your progress provides a unique alignment of the business's objectives, and sets your business up for a united and calculated approach to delivering improved financial results.

If you are like most entrepreneurs, you have been frustrated with many aspects of your business:

- No financial clarity
- No formal strategic direction
- No clear path to realizing financial progress
- Not having good financial information available to make informed decisions

In addition, this leaves you with questions to be answered like:

- Is my business actually making money?
- Where did all the cash go?
- Are we are paying too much tax?
- Are we spending too much money on major expenses like payroll?
- How do I make more money in my business?

Here is the good news, if you implement the Vision to Results framework, your frustrations will be eliminated, and your questions will be answered.

In addition, by implementing the Vision to Results framework, you will have:

- A formal outline of the financial vision of your business
- An intimate understanding of how your financial model works, and how to positively impact your business's future profitability
- A financial projection of what your business's future financial success looks like
- An outline of what critical drivers will have the greatest impact in driving financial results
- A financial scoreboard created so that you always know how your business is performing
- An understanding of how your business can stay accountable to its financial goals by implementing a meeting schedule that works

In addition, you will understand how to:

- Maximize your business's profitability
- Improve your business's cash flow
- Minimize future tax liabilities
- Create wealth at an exponential rate

The only question remaining will be do I implement this process myself, or do I hire someone to implement it for me? This answer to this question is ... it depends on your specific situation. But here is what I know:

"Doing the same thing over and over again but expecting different results is the definition of insanity."
— Albert Einstein

Whatever approach you decide on, the reality is that you need to take action now to secure the financial future of your business and implement your Vision to Results program to realize extraordinary financial results.

As I have mentioned a few times in this book, I take great pleasure in working with some of the world's brightest and most successful entrepreneurs. Our team works with these entrepreneurs to implement the Vision to Results framework into their business, creating financial clarity and driving exponential financial results very quickly. In fact, in working with our team, several of our clients have been recognized as some of the fastest growing companies in North America.

If you decide that you want to take immediate action and have our team set you up for achieving immediate results, here is how we can help:

- **WORK WITH US** – If you want to work with our team directly to implement this framework in your business and to accelerate your realization of extraordinary financial results, click here to book an appointment with our team – https://www.scheduleyou.in/qmuaez

- **CONNECT WITH US** – If you are not quite ready to implement, but want to stay in touch with us and follow us on social media channels, check out the following resources:
  - www.GauvreauCPA.ca
  - Facebook – @GauvreauCPA
  - Instagram – @GauvreauCPA
  - Twitter – @GauvreauCPA
  - LinkedIn – https://ca.linkedin.com/in/robert-gauvreau-fcpa-fca-93531430

o Regardless of how you want to do it, commit to taking the first step toward taking control of your business by taking massive action and starting the process toward realizing extraordinary financial results.

CHAPTER 16:

Financial Freedom

"True wealth is the ability to live life on your own terms. It's freedom. Money itself isn't wealth, it's a vehicle – a tool you can use to achieve financial freedom, to go after the dreams you didn't think were possible, to design your life in a way that makes you feel alive and fulfilled.
The only way to achieve success is to take massive, determined actions."
– Tony Robbins

At this point you are probably eager to get started implementing the Vision to Results framework, to make more money, make a bigger impact, and provide for a future of wealth and financial freedom for you and your family. Let's get started.

How to implement the six steps of the Vision to Results framework:

1. **Start with the End in Mind**

   Start with outlining your vision for your business, outlining specific goals and objectives you want to accomplish in the future. You will need to outline how much money you want to make, what you want to want to accomplish with your business, what impact you want to have with your business, and what resources you need in order to accomplish your vision.

Your vision becomes clear when you hold your goal-setting session that establishes your entrepreneurial purpose and the people (and culture) you need for success, and defines your positioning or competitive advantage over your competition.

You need to be clear on what your goals are in ten years, in five years, in three years, and in one year. Once you have outlined your major targets, you will have a clear vision of what you need to do today in order to realize your financial vision.

2. Understand Your Financial Model

For your business to be successful, you need to understand what your desired profit is, what the costs associated with generating these profits are, and what revenue you need to deliver in order for your desired profits to be realized.

In addition, you need to understand the profitability related to the product or service you are delivering to your clients, what the impacts on the company profitability are should the revenue increase or decrease, what the fixed costs associated with delivering your revenue look like, and what resources you need to be brought in to ensure the quality deliver to your customers.

3. Predicting Financial Results

It is essential that you understand and visually see the desired financial results of your business. In fact, how can you know if you are on track to reaching your financial goals if the goals aren't clearly outlined ahead of time?

When predicting your desired financial results, it is important that you start with the end in mind, meaning, start with how much profit you want to make at the end of the day. I have a document to help you that provides the steps you need to implement this process, which can be found at gauvreaucpa.ca/the-wealthy-entrepreneur/resources. From there, you need to outline your fixed costs, understand what gross profit your company needs to deliver, and know what the overall sales targets are. You can download the sales mix document at www.gauvreaucpa.ca/the-wealthy-enterpreneur/resources/. Once this is completed, you have a big picture target to see what needs to be accomplished to reach your financial goals.

4. Outline Key Business Drivers

Once you have outlined the high-level financial objectives of your organization through the budgeting process, you need to outline the individual metrics that need to be accomplished in order for your budgeted financial results to be realized. This starts with outlining the accountability of each element of your business, starting with the three main components: marketing, operations, and finance.

Once you understand the overall organization accountability chart, you need to dive a little bit deeper and understand the one person who is responsible for each area of the business and what their three to seven S.M.A.R.T. (specific, measurable, attainable, realistic, timely) goals are so that every member of your team knows exactly what needs to happen for the business's success to occur.

5. Create a Financial Scoreboard

If you want to understand the score of the game, especially

147

with the complexity of so many moving parts within a business, you need to implement a financial scoreboard. Having an up-to-date financial scoreboard for your business is essential, not only to make good financial decisions, but also to realize financial success in your business. As technology continues to advance and artificial intelligence and cloud-based solutions become more sophisticated, it is becoming easier to find a solution that fits with your organization and is easy to implement to make your financial scoreboard a reality.

The main objective here is to find a solution and connect your accounts so that it is a live scoreboard, and to ensure you have the necessary resources in place to keep it current and up-to-date. Having an up-to-date financial scoreboard is necessary for making effective strategic decisions. By implementing this tool, you will have an increased sense of awareness and will be ready to take your business to the next level.

6. Stay Accountable

If you outline your goals, outline the pathway to financial success, and keep an up-to-date scoreboard of how your business is performing, you are almost there. The only thing left is to stay accountable to your goals. Meaning, all the tools are all in place, now you just need to deliver. This all starts with the scheduling of accountability sessions to ensure everyone is delivering on the key drivers of the business.

The meeting schedule should involve quick daily huddles, weekly leadership team meetings, monthly financial reviews, quarterly strategic planning sessions, and a quarterly vision relay meeting, where you keep your team up to speed on the direction of the company and what opportunities lie ahead in the future.

Additional Steps:

For increased value beyond the six steps to implementing the Vision to Results framework, I shared with you some other key factors to realizing financial success that you need to ensure are in place, should you want to grow your business, increase your profitability, improve your cash flow, mitigate your tax burden, and build wealth. Each of these additional steps, if properly implemented, will ensure the structure is in place to allow for your business to make more money, make a bigger impact, and will provide for a future of wealth and financial freedom for you and your family.

Vision to Results – The Framework

As I have previously mentioned, I have had the great honour to work with some of the greatest entrepreneurs in the world who are making a massive difference in the lives of those they serve. A common issue that most entrepreneurs face is their inability to integrate structure, predictability, and strong financial clarity in their business. My goal with creating the Vision to Results framework is to share a simple process that, when implemented into your business, will eliminate financial uncertainty, will help you set your vision, will help you to stay on track to realizing your goals, will keep you accountable to your goals, and will generate extraordinary financial results.

I want you to understand how your business is performing so that you have a clear roadmap to earning more money, having more impact, and living a life of financial clarity and freedom.

It has been a true pleasure to serve you and provide you with my life's experience and work. Whether it be on your own or working with our team, I hope you fully implement the Vision to Results framework and realize extraordinary financial results.

Thank You

From the bottom of my heart, thank you for reading *The Wealthy Entrepreneur: The Formula for Making Money and Gaining Financial Clarity in Your Business.* I am truly grateful for the opportunity to share my 'Vision to Results' framework with you and am committed to offering as many insights as I can to help you achieve future financial freedom! At the same time, I would like to congratulate you for taking the first step toward making positive financial change, and for striving to increase the impact of your business. It is entrepreneurs like you that will continue to successfully change the world, and it is people like you that continue to inspire me every day!

I would like to welcome you to a private Facebook group I have created for entrepreneurs just like you, so that I can continue to support you on your journey, and so that entrepreneurs like you and I can continue to inspire each other and achieve even greater results in the future.

Here is the link to request access to the group:

https://www.facebook.com/groups/gauvreaucpa

I look forward to connecting with you there!

I am so grateful to work with some of the world's greatest entre-preneurs, and would love to help support you in any way that I can. If you feel that connecting for a thirty-minute call would help support your mission, I would be happy to connect. Feel free to schedule a time with me on my schedule below:

gauvreaucpa.ca/the-wealthy-entrepreneur/resources.

Thank you once again for being part of my journey, and I look forward to welcoming you into my community.

About the Author

Robert Gauvreau is a FCPA who works exclusively with entrepreneurs and professionals to help them make more money and gain financial clarity in their businesses. As a financial expert and bestselling author, Robert shares his insight and wisdom as a public speaker, is often cited in major business journals related to money, finances, and entrepreneurship, and works directly with more than 500 business across North America, helping them build better businesses and generate greater financial performance.

As an undergraduate student, Robert studied business with a focus on human resources at Trent University, and graduated in 2005 with a Bachelor of Business Administration degree (BBA). From there, Robert continued his studies at the University of Toronto, Rotman School of Business, where Robert completed a master's degree in management and professional accounting (MMPA). Upon completing his graduate degree in 2006, Robert began working with a leading global accounting firm that focused on providing assurance services to large non-profit organizations and government agencies. It was through this experience that Robert qualified as a CPA in Ontario, Canada and received his professional designation in 2008.

While working at the global accounting firm, Robert realized his passion was working with entrepreneurs and professionals. In 2008, Robert founded a new CPA firm to focus on helping entrepreneurs and professionals make more money and gain financial clarity in their businesses. Robert founded Gauvreau CPA on three core values: people, passion, and integrity. Robert has grown this business from a startup to a multimillion-dollar tax and advisory firm that is committed to delivering a proactive approach to accounting and tax services while delivering exceptional client service. Robert and his team have quickly become one of North America's leading tax and advisory firms focused on entrepreneurs and have been recognized as one of Canada's fastest-growing professional services firms.

Since 2008, Robert has been recognized with numerous awards and achievements, including being admitted into fellowship with CPA Canada in 2018, being admitted into the Greater Peterborough Business Hall of Fame in 2018, being recognized with an alumni leadership award from Trent University in 2018, and many other business excellence and professional services awards.

In 2016, Robert and three partners founded a 38,000 square foot business hub in Peterborough Ontario called Venture North, devoted to helping entrepreneurs and small businesses find the resources, support, and guidance they need to thrive and succeed in the business world. Since its inception, Venture North has been home to thousands of startup businesses, and continues to introduce new initiatives to support the success of these local and global entrepreneurial initiatives.

Robert lives in Peterborough, Ontario Canada with his wife Jenny and their two children Jack and Sophia, and continues to devote significant time toward working with charities and non-profit organizations, and giving back to the community that has provided him with such great opportunity.

Gauvreau CPA

Website: http://GauvreauCPA.ca
Facebook: https://www.facebook.com/gauvreaucpa
Twitter: https://twitter.com/gauvreaucpa
LinkedIn: https://www.linkedin.com/company/gauvreaucpa
Instagram: https://www.instagram.com/gauvreaucpa

Personal

Email: bgauvreau@gauvreaucpa.ca
Facebook: https://www.facebook.com/bob.gauvreau.1
Twitter: https://twitter.com/robert_gauvreau
LinkedIn: https://ca.linkedin.com/in/
robert-gauvreau-fcpa-fca-93531430
Instagram: https://www.instagram.com/robertgauvreau/

CPSIA information can be obtained
at www.ICGtesting.com
Printed in the USA
BVHW040540310321
603715BV00004B/7/J